HYDROPONIC PATH
AMID CLIMATE WRATH

Hydroponics Pays Back in a Year.
The Money Path. The Money Spinner.
+ Untold Climate Truths Unveiled.

Vivek Aggarwal

ISBN
Paperback 979-8-89556-970-2
Hardcase 979-8-89610-747-7

Hydroponics - The Money Path to Riches

Payback in a year...
Could there be a better venture?
All the hydroponic secrets revealed.

Climate - Why Aren't Our Climate Initiatives Working?

Untold, eye-opening climate revelations.
Mysteries of the Environment.
A novel approach, a wholesome experience.

Environment... our primary benevolent benefactor.

Environment... all-encompassing, omniscient... munificent.

Environment... Enraged!

Contents

Acknowledgments

Where should this start and end!

This book fructifies as a product of a learning journey that's as old as my existence. All aspects that brought me into being deserve acknowledgment, most pertinently the 3 tall pillars - Parents who strived to provide beyond their means – as is the universal truth; Family & Friends who shape our thoughts & character - apart from being our personal safety net; Professional fraternity that contributes to our furtherance. Every other person we meet & interact with is a teacher. Even without interaction, we receive influence from the environment – the book gets to that mystery in the end.

I thank my entire environment, seen and unseen, that shapes our destiny, as it did in the culmination of this book.

Specifically, Kartik, always a step ahead, introduced me to hydroponics when it was unheard of.

My wife, Aparna, did the most difficult task for her - remaining quiet for the countless hours when I was engrossed in creating this book.

My wonderful sons, Vinayak & Mayank; my sister Vandana and Tarun G; my support circuit.

Kamal & Ritesh for their support and novel thoughts that helped create some of our ingenious products.

Anupam, Kapil, Mahendra, Shyam, Srinivas, Soumya, Vikas, Manoj, Manish, Gullu, and Aryan Patel.

Samarvir, Shailesh, Ashish... and my entire IIT-BHU gang.

Suhail Mathur for his publishing guidance.

My writer friends Chittranjan Pathak and Swarnendu Bhushan.

First, the book briefly discusses untold climate truths.

Balance is all in Hydroponics.

Ends with Some Mysteries of the Environment.

Please Do <u>Not</u> Skip.

Start from the FOREWORD. It's Important.

Foreword

"In any moment of decision, the best thing you can do is the right thing, the next best thing is the wrong thing, and the worst thing you can do is nothing." Theodore Roosevelt.

Life is an iterative journey. An individual may make thousands of minor decisions every day in every walk of life. Minor decisions are typically guided by prejudice, prior experience, or a certain pre-established thought process. These minor decisions are pre-programmed and instinctive, like brushing teeth in the morning, but still, they are decisions. One may choose to do or may choose to skip.

Major decisions involve a long-term impact and have consequences of the choice one makes. Such decisions involve deeper deliberations and evaluation. Selecting one way or the other can potentially alter the course of one's life.

You have taken a decision to pick this book. So far, it's a happening, an occurrence – perhaps by chance or by reference. You happened to chance upon this book and decided to read through to gauge its purpose and its usefulness for yourself. It's a chance, a happening that you are now evaluating… contemplating and in the process, you are deciding whether it's worth your time. Decisions are neither wrong nor right. Decisions are a direction that one chooses. Making those decisions right or wrong is in one's hand to a certain extent, and of course the environment has influence. Any decision when acted upon in the right earnest, has the potential to become right. Decisions need to be acted upon, for them to fructify into desirable outcomes. Decision requires application of self & resources, to mature those decisions into a journey that culminates toward a destination where one intends to be.

Now, if you happen to read through the book and get motivated enough to pursue the hydroponic path - to reap its riches or joy, would you say you were just plain lucky by chancing upon this book, or was it the application of yourself that converted a random happening into an opportunity? Would you be inclined to infer it as serendipity, or would you be more inclined to credit it to your application thereof? Or was there something more to it? After we have done discussing Climate and hydroponics, we'll discuss 'Environment mysteries' in the end — some intriguing scientific & parapsychological experiments related to us - all factual — all scientific - that are proven to impact our individual destiny & actions, but remain mysteries yet. Aspects that are beyond the common domain and will force one to think. About how the opportunities may be coming or lurking by our way, and we may not be tapping into them, blissfully unaware as we stroll by. I was lucky to have been introduced to hydroponics by my nephew Kartik, by chance. Was I plain lucky? Or did I manage to make it into a 'lucky' break - by acting upon the information that chanced upon my way? Don't we come across such tips in life all the time when we are conversing & interacting with our environment in the vicinity? What makes some people lucky — are they born lucky or can luck be cultivated? We'll come to all that in the end.

How many business ventures can one think of, where payback can be as little as a year, and investment returns in just a year? That's where hydroponics stands out. Hydroponics is extremely profitable if done right, and the book tells how to do it just right – as a profession or just as a prolific hobby.

Hydroponics is the art of profusely growing all kinds of veggies-easily-without soil-without fields-free of pesticides-with hugely accelerated growth-free of weather vagaries, commercial or hobby.

That's hydroponics... an acquired taste.

This book is an easily comprehensible & practical presentation. Everything possible about hydroponics is disclosed in plain language to arm the reader with comprehensive know-how to pursue successful and profitable hydroponics as a profession or as a hobby. Before plunging into hydroponics, the book explains the scientific and logical rationale behind this pursuit.

Hydroponic profitability improves as the climate gets harsher, as it will! The book presents surprising facts about why our climate initiatives aren't working, some hitherto unknown, untold, and factual aspects of climate change... eye-opening.

The book endeavors to ensure the reader's time is well spent, more enlightened – with a wholesome knowledge-sharing and reading experience like a novel. Attempting to be interesting as well as empowering, potentially life-enhancing, striving to be that one book that must be read.

Setting the Tune

It was sometime in the year 2017 when my nephew Kartik had come over to stay with us for a few days, his visit always like a festival… keenly awaited. We were dining when he initiated a conversation.

"Mama, do you know plants can be grown without soil?"

I knew Kartik had a knack for exploring knowledge beyond the ordinary, always expecting him to possess more than conventionally conspicuous wisdom. But the idea of growing plants without soil seemed too far-fetched… fantastical!

I just rolled my eyes, ignored him and continued with my dinner.

Unfazed, he giggled and baited me.

"Actually, plants can be grown just in thin air."

I looked up to meet his eyes, trying to discern if there could be a modicum of seriousness.

"Of course, elephants can fly!"

His enthusiasm didn't wane; instead, it got fueled as a gleeful chuckle spread across his expression.

"You don't believe me, right?"

Let me give some credence to the child's fantasy, I naively thought, and said,

"OK, suppose it's possible, why would one do it?"

Still smiling, he responded,

"If I say it's a goldmine, will that be a valid reason?"

Without playing me further, he obliged,

"OK, Mama… just google hydroponics."

While I searched him with incredulous looks, my wife Aparna, who has a research background in Tissue Culture, chirped, *"Well, we used to grow potatoes in the lab on medium."*

Medium, hydroponics, plants growing in air… why draw myself into hypotheticals? I just nodded, successfully side-stepped the conversation and veered it off in some other direction that I do not recall now.

Later in the night, curiosity got the better of me, and I typed 'hydroponics' on my phone.

That was the year 2017. Seven years on, I have managed to successfully develop several unique front-runner products related to hydroponics & horticulture and am in a position to share all the hydroponic know-how - for easy application as a very profitable money-making venture, or just as a rewarding hobby.

One never knows in life from where new possibilities would emerge. Perhaps, like this book in your hands.

Direction is often and frequently shown to us by the environment, invisible and pervasive forces surrounding us and beyond ordinary comprehension. We just need to be perceptive and receptive to the directions, and then be reactive to act on those directions with an open mind. That, I believe, is life's way and purpose. In this context, we'll discuss some very interesting Mysteries of the Environment, all scientific and related to how the environment may be shaping our actions, our destiny – briefly discussed in the end, in a purely factual way.

Knowledge never goes to waste. Knowledge is like ascending steps; one leads to another, thereby magnifying and further opening new learning doors. My interest in acquiring hydroponic information and converting it into commercial ventures opened several more learning paths progressively. I got to understand how to establish supply chains and how to deal with suppliers. Website & App development has intricacies of their own, and getting them made within budget has nuances that one grapples with before grasping while on the job. Erstwhile esoteric subjects like HSN, Trademarks, Patents, GST, SEO, CPC, ACOS, etc., became all too familiar. Difficult to believe it myself, recently I learned to design using AI!

Beyond our usual occupations, it's an interesting world out there waiting to be discovered if we are receptive to the environment. That's the purpose of this book - to introduce an interesting and lesser-known source of immense empowerment - hydroponics, through a novel-like reading experience.

Hydroponic Ventures Are Money Spinners.

If you were asked to enumerate some other businesses that can pay back the entire investment in a year or so, without risk, without years of learning, without sweat on brow, without deep pockets… how many could you manage to enumerate? Probably none.

Hydroponic ventures offer all that, and more.

Why isn't everyone doing it, then?

Some are, many more will.

Genuine knowledge is the missing key.

Commonly, people tend to refer free online information – that's grossly lacking.

This book provides genuine knowledge, the key differentiator, to profitably do it.

Have you heard of Ashwin Sawant? He's an entrepreneur in Pune who became a hydroponic millionaire.

Another millionaire, Vivek Raj Poojary, featured in Forbes India for his pioneering indoor hydroponic farms growing saffron and medicinal plants.

Hydroponics will continue to become even more profitable as the climate worsens. Climate change is propelling the growth of hydroponics ventures worldwide. Misery opens opportunity paths too – the truth of life.

First, we'll briefly discuss climate – but beyond the commonly propagated narrative. That's very interesting. Climate change is known to everybody, but barely understood. First, for the discerning reader, alternative perspectives are presented regarding where the real climate issues lie… the elephant in the room… and what supplementary efforts need to be applied to effectively rein in the climate change, for which some surprisingly unknown aspects will be unveiled related to the current buzzword 'Global Warming'.

Our current climate efforts are not working, visible amply to everyone. In the year 2024, our world has already crossed the temperature threshold that we had aimed never to cross[1], with the year 2023 being the hottest ever on record. Alarms are blaring and turning red all around us, too obvious to remain oblivious. The climate impact has eventually become too adverse to be dismissed & ignored any further as an event.

It is a phenomenon.

Climate change is not a phenomenon that is occurring somewhere in a far distance, from which one can remain aloof. This is not a subject confined within the boundaries of a few states or nations.

This is the single most prominent matter that directly & distinctly affects every single person living on Earth, and actually decides the survivability of the progeny.

In the Mahabharat epic, there is a story where, after all his brothers were killed by the Yaksha (a kind of Demigod said to protect an important resource), it fell upon Yudhishthira to answer the Yaksha's questions in order to revive his slain brothers and gain access to the water body protected by the Yaksha. Yudhishthira was the most intelligent of the 5 famous Pandava brothers. One of the questions that the Yaksha asked was, "What is truly amazing in this world?" to which Yudhishthira replied, "*The most amazing thing is, though humans are mortal, everybody goes about their life as if they are going to be here forever.*"

Today, to the same question, Yudhishthira might have replied differently, in my opinion, perhaps saying, "*The most amazing thing is, though the world is getting hotter every day, everybody goes about their life as if it is for someone else to bear.*"

Real answers to climate redressal come first in the book, real reasons why it isn't working. Our current focus on 'emissions reduction' is only a part of the solution. The real issues lie elsewhere, amazingly unaddressed – that's explained first.

The first 15% of the book is about untold climate truths.

Balance is all about hydroponics, with some interesting Mysteries of the Environment in the end.

The climate portion is eye-opening... guaranteed!

But if in a tearing hurry, the reader may go straight to hydroponics.

—————❖❖—————

Chapter 1

Climate

In the year 2024, our world has already crossed the temperature threshold that we had aimed never to cross[1], with the year 2023 being the hottest ever on record.

All our contemporary climate remediation initiatives are designed to prevent global temperature excursion beyond 1.5 degrees Celsius compared to pre-industrial levels by 2100. This is the foundation on which all current climate policies are formulated and promulgated. Despite all climate initiatives in this direction of preventing temperature increase beyond 1.5 degrees Celsius, the world already breached the mark in March 2024!

Ice glaciers are retreating. Polar ice sheets are thinning. Oceans are getting warmer and sea levels rising. Closer home, for the first time ever, the temperature in Delhi kissed 50 degrees Celsius in May 2024. Morocco is seeing its sixth straight year of drought in 2024, and its huge Al Massira reservoir has dried down to just 3% of its original volume in less than a decade[2]. The Mediterranean's olive plantations are drying up and losing production by half, due to difficult weather conditions in Europe[3]. The viability of olive production has become a concern. Saffron production is becoming dearer with reducing yields[4]. Corals are bleaching more frequently and rampantly from Australia to Thailand, forcing the closure of beaches[5]. Dubai is seeing repeated flooding. Parts of deserts like Saudi Arabia have started reeling under floods. Weather events have become more extreme and unimaginable.

Alarms are blaring and turning red all around us, too obvious to remain oblivious.

Climate change and its potent impact have now become a life reality and are no longer confined to disjointed events.

It's a phenomenon.

Fact of life is, climate is a subject that is largely left to coteries of policymakers or higher echelons of governance, where unfortunately, policy decisions may be influenced by parochial interests. Hence, the end result... a cipher... we've already crossed the temperature threshold we aimed never to cross, i.e. to prevent global temperature rise beyond 1.5 degrees Celsius compared to pre-industrial levels.

Why aren't our climate efforts working?

In as simple parlance as possible, we discuss here the reasons why it isn't working. Alternative radical views are put forward toward what needs to be done to make it work and the radical remediations that the world must undertake – both at society and individual levels. Global consciousness in climate matters is evidently lacking among the common populace, understandably so, as the subject is perceived as being too esoteric by the masses. Ask anyone what should be done to rein in global warming and in all probability, the response, if any, would revolve around switching from fossil fuel consumption to electric vehicles. That's not incorrect, but vastly inadequate. The common person's perception on the subject is grossly limited, so patently an individual person cannot contribute much to make any impact.

Dendrobium orchid is a beautiful flower - flaming bright yellow in color - that's endemic to Taiwan[6]. Clumps of these flowers grow on unbranched green stems of the plant. Local Tsou tribes revere it as the God Flower, as it is an essential constituent in the worship rituals for them. As their belief goes, God wouldn't be able to find them unless they have this flower in the ceremonies. These flowers grow in a warm climate but need a cold winter to form buds that can then bloom in springtime. This flower used to be omnipresent at one point in time in Taiwan. But now, it requires some serious exploratory efforts by indigenous people to be able to find it. With increasing global temperatures, this flower has become scarce - climate change is taking its toll. The indigenous Tsou tribes worry how would their God find them without this flower? For them, no Dendrobium orchid flower means God can't arrive at their ceremonies. Ensconced in our material world, it will be very difficult for a city dweller to understand that this flower has become a kind of existential crisis for this tribe. Different aspects of life are valued differently by different sets of people, the point here being that climate change is significantly impacting everyone – from remote tribes to city dwellers - everyone.

Reality is all the current climate initiatives are hardly making a dent.

They are barely enough, and as a result, it's slipping away from our hands.

This initial part of the book brings forth the basic underlying issue regarding climate that has shockingly gone unnoticed – deliberately or through ignorance, and hence remained unaddressed. The climate situation will not improve only by leaders. It will now require the common person to become instrumental in climate aspects, to be able to start contributing effectively and possibly to start influencing the policies. That's what this part of the book aims to achieve - through climate-related knowledge empowerment of the common man. It will take time, for just a book does not change the world. Let's at least begin our progression in that direction.

Despite bringing these climate realities in this book, it's known that the world will go on as it currently is… rapidly plummeting further toward harsher climate. So, we do the next best thing – to reap its advantage! The harsher the climate, even more profitable hydroponics would continue to become, making it future-proof. Let's get to understand the esoteric & unknown climate change-related aspects first, then we'll begin with hydroponics.

Natural Cycles

Who is primarily responsible for climate change?

Humans or God?

If humans are responsible, what would have happened if we had not changed the climate?

If Gods are responsible, how can we, the puny humans, make an impact contrary to God's intent?

Thankfully, science and logic have the answers.

Refer to the following chart, which is unique and rare, and shows what has been happening to the Earth for the past *8 lakh years*.

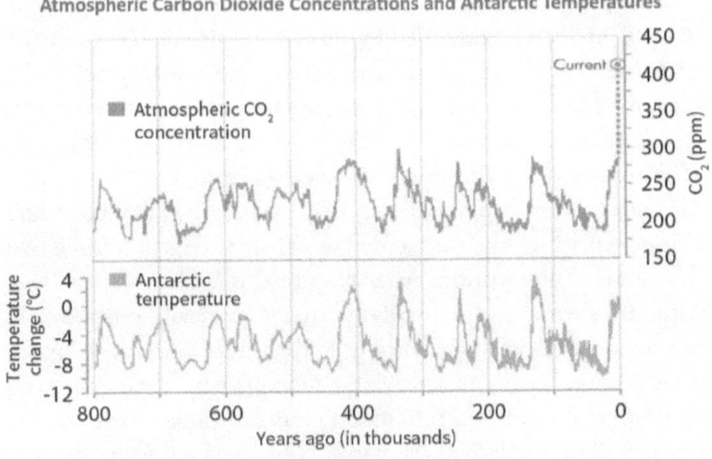

Source: United States Environmental Protection Agency. [7]
www.epa.gov/climatechange-science/causes-climate-change

This point needs re-emphasis, lest it escaped the attention – that this chart is talking about happenings over the last 'several *lakhs*' of years – 800,000 years – nearly a millennium – all scientifically established, while the current form of intelligent humans appeared only a couple of thousand years ago.

Understandably, it would be inconceivable how data of the past 800,000 years can be found! It appears to be a bluff. But that's the beauty of science. This remarkable chart is developed thanks to astounding research at the USA's Antarctica stations, specifically the National Oceanic & Atmospheric Administration (NOAA)[7,8,9]. Antarctic ice that had been depositing for millions of years was drilled out gradually, carefully, and sequentially in the form of ice cores – like ice cylinders - from up to three-kilometers underground. The ancient air bubbles trapped inside these Antarctic ice cores were analyzed to find the composition of that ancient air that would have been millions of years back. Purely ingenious! If you'd been wondering what the scientists do at Antarctic Stations in bone-biting cold, this is one of the many wonderful things they do.

This chart shows clearly that the Earth has always been in a cyclic state of upheaval every 50 thousand years or so. Crests in the chart are the points where Carbon Dioxide (CO_2) reaches the maximum, and then the CO_2 falls back to a minimum in the next couple of thousand years. The CO_2 rises again in the next couple of thousand years, and then falls back again in a cyclic manner. All this has been happening naturally over the last 800,000 years at least, for which the chart could be constructed. All this *without* any human intervention. According to this graph, life has been naturally created and naturally destroyed cyclically every couple of thousand years – without any human intervention. A logical presumption here is that it wasn't humans who were appearing cyclically every couple of thousand years to run fancy cars and to finish it all off the face of the Earth. Now, notice the end portion of the chart. It can be seen that the Carbon Dioxide (CO_2) has spiked and suddenly become too high for comfort. This spike has indeed been caused by humans, while all the earlier cycles were caused naturally.

For the skeptics of climate change, this chart is a scientific historical proof that Carbon Dioxide (CO_2) and global temperatures go hand in hand. The more CO_2 in the atmosphere, the higher the atmospheric temperature – as clearly seen by the overlapping peaks and troughs of this chart. Peaks of high CO_2 coincide with the peaks of atmospheric temperatures, and the troughs of low CO_2 coincide with the lows of atmospheric temperatures. There is an element of doubt regarding cause and effect. Does the rising CO_2 in the atmosphere *cause* enhanced air temperature, or is it the other way around – meaning CO_2 may not be the cause; rather, it may serve as feedback to amplify changes initiated by other cosmic initiators. All our current theories are based on consideration of the former, that rising CO_2 in the atmosphere leads to enhanced air temperature, and this is the theory substantiated and supported by almost all of the scientific community. So, we'll subscribe to it.

This chart is also proof of natural cataclysmic cycles, showing that life has flourished and perished in a cyclic manner over the past thousands of centuries. To some, this can serve as proof to support the theory that some religions profess, that creation and destruction are part of natural heavenly cycles. We could marvel at the striking similarity between scientific studies and the contents of our religious texts, but we do not want to head in that direction.

Hence, the question that comes forth is, before humans appeared on this planet, what was causing these rhythmic life cycles - causing the cyclical increases in air temperatures? What was the reason that changed the global temperature cyclically over the past 800,000 years, when humans were not around in earlier eons to pollute?

The cyclical creation of life and its natural destruction as a natural phenomenon, irrespective of the presence of humans, is easy to understand if simple logic is applied. This cyclical phenomenon happens because the sun has continuously kept supplying solar radiation endlessly since pre-history. Part of the solar radiation bounces off and a part gets through into our atmosphere to heat up the planet differentially between landmasses and oceans. As the planet heats up, temperatures increase. As the temperature increases, more CO_2 gets liberated from oceans and ice melts. More CO_2 in the atmosphere leads to further warming and more increase in sea level, and a point comes when the sea inundates land and finishes it all off to bring down the temperatures. And the cycle repeats. It keeps repeating irrespective of human presence.

Tons of research has been conducted on the subject and the reason for these cycles is generally explained as Milankovitch cycles[8]. Milankovitch cycles are very complex to understand, so we'll discuss them in just 2-3 paragraphs – lest it becomes boring. Leaving aside the intricate technicalities, Milankovitch cycles are ups and downs seen on the chart - caused due to external influences on Earth leading to periodic cyclical changes in Earth's tilt (Obliquity), Orbit's eccentricity, and Precession (wobble of Earth's axis). External influences here mean the cosmic-level influences, like those by other celestial bodies viz. stars. Due to the cyclical changes in Earth's tilt and orbital patterns, ice cover in high latitude areas gets impacted and ice cover grows in these areas. Ice doesn't generate from nothing. It comes from the water of oceans that evaporates and transforms into ice to deposit on land. The transfer of water from oceans into ice starts reducing the sea levels. During the peak of earlier ice ages, sea levels are known to fall around a huge 120 meters compared to current levels. Reducing sea levels expose the land, where vegetation grows by consuming carbon dioxide (CO_2) from the atmosphere, hence reducing air temperatures coincide with reducing CO_2 in the air. Colder oceans and other associated events due to cool air temperatures further absorb the CO_2 from the air. Such sponging of CO_2 out of the air further amplifies this cooling phenomenon. The cycle then repeats in reverse.

If it's too much to grasp, just understand that Milankovitch cycles are caused by external cosmic factors that change the Earth's tilt and rotating patterns – naturally, and that impacts the distribution of solar heat between land and sea, thereby changing air temperatures. Cyclically. Naturally.

Periodic cyclical changes in the Earth's orbital patterns are the major external factors that regularly and cyclically change the distribution of solar radiation received between the Earth's northern and southern hemispheres, leading to a cyclical redistribution of water and ice between the 2 hemispheres. This redistribution further impacts the reflectivity of the Earth's surface, the ocean's ability to absorb CO_2, and the release of more landmass where vegetation grows and absorbs more CO_2. The overall outcome of this hugely complex phenomenon is that these cyclical changes repeat every 50,000 years or so and are a result of a cosmic-level play.

The most important point that comes out of looking at the past 800,000 years is that global warming has always been present; it occurs cyclically every 50,000 years or so.

But mind you, that doesn't absolve humans.

Humans are surely the culprits in so much that we have hastened the warming this time round – primarily by digging out fossil fuels and burning them. Recent human intervention has spiked the CO_2 levels to unprecedented highs – as evident from the far right of the chart presented above, where the spike in CO_2 and the atmospheric temperatures is both evident.

The fact that this human interference has impacted and countered the celestial play of things that have been going on since ages is astounding. This is an interesting cosmic-level feat by humans, though not to be congratulated as it has tilted the cyclic balance toward harm's way. The human activities leading to the accumulation of CO_2 and other greenhouse gases in the atmosphere are rightfully disdained - as it has led to the current bout of 'Global warming,' as so often heard. For the uninitiated, greenhouse gases are those gases that prevent the solar radiation from reflecting back - out of the Earth's atmosphere. Carbon Dioxide (CO_2) is the most prominent greenhouse gas that is the subject of everyone's focus… rightly so as it kind of bounces back the reflected solar radiation that was trying to leave the Earth's atmosphere. There are other greenhouse gases too – especially the chlorofluorocarbons that are used in air-conditioning equipment – they are hundreds of times more potent greenhouse gases compared to CO_2. It may be surprising to know that actually water vapor is also a greenhouse gas. Water vapor in the atmosphere has 4 times more potent greenhouse effect compared to carbon dioxide, but the good part is that water condenses and does not keep accumulating in the atmosphere. Water goes through condensation cycles and precipitates out of the air. Water actually absorbs the surface heat to vaporize and transfers it to higher atmospheric levels during condensation, helping it escape out. Thereby, water is not considered for its greenhouse impact, even though it's debated in some circles. Methane is another greenhouse gas that is even more dangerous - up to 84 times more potent than CO_2 and will be talked about later.

As a result of human activities, the global warming cycle has been extended and aggravated this time round – as is evident from the peak seen on the rightmost portion of the chart. Currently, CO_2 levels hover around 420, while historically even a CO_2 level of just 300 was sufficient to trigger changes in our world – repeatedly! Why has nature been so benevolent this time round and not triggered even though we have surpassed the earlier triggering points? It's already been quite some time since the last upheaval as per the chart – observe the gap between the peaks, giving the impression that we've already outlived our time from the last peak! If humans had not intervened, it is well evident from this chart that a cooling cycle was overdue, and we would have started our descent toward an ice age. Research shows that global warming due to human intervention has postponed the ice age to the right – by anywhere between a few thousand to hundreds of thousands of years![10]. That's actually a very positive side-effect of human activity – having postponed the ice age by several thousand years; otherwise, we would have been struggling to thaw ourselves out of the freeze. In fact, one way to look at it is that human-induced global warming has prevented us from hurtling down the path toward the next impending cyclic ice age. But hold on… let's not start congratulating ourselves.

Excess of anything hurts, as the adage goes.

If something's good, it's not necessary that it will remain good for eternity.

Value and utility of everything change depending on the circumstances and environment.

Human-induced global warming has served our interests by postponing the next impending cyclic ice age by a few thousand years. That is a boon of human activity. However, in the current timeframe and foreseeable future, human-induced global warming has become a bane of gargantuan proportions. Excessive human activity has severely interfered with the natural Milankovitch cycles, and now we are in for a really long and very hot summer period for the coming centuries, at the very least.

So, to live on, we now really need to go down our chosen path to rein in the climate change… lest we boil ourselves away. A contrarian thought process can be that if the environment has been self-correcting for the past 800,000 years at least, as evident from cycles in the chart, so should happen this time round too. So why worry? The environment is indeed responding. As the world gets warmer, we are already seeing that newer and previously undiscovered aspects of climate are now coming to the fore. Never did we hear about the 'flying rivers' [25], did we? Recent research in the US, Germany, and IITs in India has discovered a new kind of weather phenomenon wherein massive unimaginable ribbons of heavy water vapor get generated from oceans due to exaggerated heating caused by global warming, and these heavy water-laden ribbons traverse across thousands of miles on land, before suddenly dropping their entire load in the form of sudden deluge - extremely heavy localized downpour - a devastating river originating from the sky that obliterates whatever comes in its path. We all have heard about cloudbursts earlier, but this phenomenon is another dimension of things as they have started happening now. These massive ribbons, also called atmospheric rivers, are gargantuan beings – 2000 to 5000 km long, 500 km wide and nearly 3 km deep and research says these are getting bigger every next time they occur. To get the perspective, these ribbons may contain double the flow as in the Amazon River - the world's largest river by the discharge volume of water. Imagine double the flow of such a river suddenly pounding upon a localized area, causing unimaginable landslides and washout. Nothing stays in their path. This is not fictional, rather something that's become frequent around the world. These massive ribbons remain invisible to the naked eye, but are observable through satellite imagery. This is just one erstwhile unheard of way in which the environment is responding to the human-induced part of climate change that has interfered with the Milankovitch cycles. The environment will respond for certain, to human interference, to revert toward the ancient cycles it has been following. Such newer kinds of calamities are only expected to rise in number and intensity, as time progresses. The environment's response and its own course correction would not be kind, would not be gentle. It's for this reason that humans must act seriously and do their part toward climate remediation, for to wait for the environment to do this correction for us would come with dire consequences.

One may have comprehended by now that there's so much more to climate change, compared to what is commonly narrated. Burning of fossil fuels is usually attributed as the sole reason for global warming. But there are other colossal cosmic-level factors at play – factors that are external to the Earth's atmosphere, and human comprehension of the climate affairs is rather dim. Almost nobody would have heard of the concept of Milankovitch cycles… its huge impact on climate, the fact that global warming is a historical and cyclically occurring natural phenomenon, and the fact that global warming has had some beneficial side-effects as well by pushing the ice age away.

Let's move on.

The world's climate-related initiatives are decided by the United Nations Framework Convention on Climate Change (UNFCCC). All member countries of UNFCCC hold annual meetings to collectively decide the way forward. These annual meetings are called Conference of the Parties (COP). COP28 was the 28th such meeting for the UN Climate Control body held in the year 2023, where the world came together to agree on ways to address the climate crisis, such as limiting global temperature rise to 1.5 degrees Celsius by the year 2100, and achieving net-zero emissions by 2050, by cutting down global emissions through transitioning away from fossil fuels, tripling renewable energy, and tripling nuclear energy capacity.

Noteworthy in the context is that the world has already accepted that we can only aim to reduce the temperature rise; we cannot prevent its rise or reverse it. That's factual. The world has decided to 'limit' the global temperature rise to 1.5 degrees Celsius by 2100, which is the tacit acknowledgment in this context. Being cognizant of one's limitations is actually a strength. The world is aware that the Earth is constantly bombarded by Terawatts of solar radiation, so constant heat addition to our atmosphere and its consequent heating are a way of life. Can't walk away from the sun.

Every single hour of sunlight corresponds to one year of the entire Earth's power needs. Pause for a moment to visualize its magnitude… that's a colossal amount of heat that the Earth gets inundated with every single hour! Out of all the radiation that's coming in, approximately 30% gets reflected away, and the balance of 70% enters our atmosphere to either heat us up or to convert into matter. Humans are puny by comparison, unable to play any significant role in this massive heat bombardment and retention play meted out by the cosmos. Solar heat energy impingement on Earth is a given; we can't do anything about it. Trying to reduce the greenhouse effect by decreasing carbon in the atmosphere is undoubtedly a step in the right direction. But that's a band-aid!

To be able to make a significant impact, the need of the hour is to buttress our efforts by channeling our endeavors toward supplementary paths. 'Energy' is the keyword here. It's the heat, the energy, that is the root cause of the subject. Energy that is entering our system and the energy that's being generated by us ourselves inside the system — both are contributing to heat us up. The world is already on the right path, though just ambling when the need is to sprint, to reduce greenhouse gas emissions, to improve the heat dissipation out of our atmosphere. But the energy that's being generated by us ourselves - it's astonishing there's hardly any effort in the direction of reducing the heat that humans add to the atmosphere by themselves! Reference here is made to the heat that is generated by humans through burning fuels, splitting atoms in nuclear reactors, capturing solar beams on solar panels, doing chemical conversions and so on — all sources of energy are actually either releasing the locked-up heat energy onto us, or capturing the heat that would have otherwise bounced back out of our environment.

Earth is like we are all inside a pot boiler that's getting heated from outside.

And we are heating it from inside, too, by ourselves — to fund our lifestyles.

Currently, we are heating our pot boiler house using dirty energy that generates emissions.

Now we are encouraging ourselves to heat our pot using clean energy that does not generate emissions.

Clean or dirty, the heat is going to boil us either way.

Clean energy, as a panacea to global warming, is a mirage if left to itself. It's our own selves that we end up heating with cleaner energy, getting burned irrespective of how clean the energy we might find.

Who in their right mind can imagine a world where we enhance our heating mechanisms more and more, aiming to cool ourselves down! This is too important a concept with a major impact, so let's try to comprehend this in another way – through a *Terrarium*.

Terrarium

A fair chance is that you have not heard of this term—
"Terrarium."

A terrarium is a wonderful concept wherein plants are housed inside a sealed container with soil (and microbes) inside. The container is sealed—nothing goes in or out except for sunlight and heat. And the plants inside grow, die, regrow, die, over and over again, and they live on for years, decades, in a totally self-contained manner. That's the epitome of sustainability. This is not fictional but factual, just as everything else in this book—factual, though it may appear incredible at times. Save your awe for some exceptionally incredulous scientific experiments related to the environment that we'll briefly discuss in the chapter titled

"Life Mysteries of the Environment," and they are all entirely factual, though exceedingly unbelievable.

So, a terrarium is a sealed container with soil (and microbes) inside where plants grow, and they keep dying and regrowing on their own for decades. Microbes inside feed upon the fallen leaves and dead organic matter to provide nourishment for the sustenance of new leaves to grow with the help of incoming sunlight. Oxygen and carbon dioxide get entirely recycled within this confined environment. This sealed container exchanges heat with the environment outside. Care has to be exercised so as not to let this sealed environment get too hot; caution needs to be practiced. It may be difficult to believe, but horticulture enthusiasts boast of possessing terrariums that are over a few decades old, like this one by David Latimer of the UK—amazing!

Source: Owned by David Latimer, www.weather.com/home-garden/news/thriving-garden-bottle(11)

A terrarium is a self-contained, isolated ecosystem where incoming heat evaporates the water content of the soil, and it condenses back, forming a perpetual water cycle. Plants grow using incoming sunlight and by picking up nutrients from the soil. Dead leaves drop back into the soil, where microbes devour them to turn them back into nutrients, forming a never-ending nutrient cycle.

Terrariums are small yet magical… you can hold a typical-sized terrarium in your hands, though people have made them big, too. I plan to make one myself to keep on my study desk.

But then… Why should I?

Why should I build a small Terrarium when actually I'm already living inside a Terrarium!

Whatever has just been described for a terrarium very well fits the functioning of our Earth, but on a gargantuan scale… a cosmic scale. The Earth's atmosphere is held together by gravitational forces, which provide a sealing that does not allow our atmosphere to escape into space. Only sunlight and heat can come in and out, and life inside is self-contained through the recycling of matter and gases

Our Earth is exactly a Terrarium.

Now, visualize—considering a small man-made terrarium, like the one in the image above. Imagine that the microbes living inside this small man-made terrarium decide to start a small bonfire *inside* the terrarium. This is just a fictional visualization for the purpose of understanding. Visualization expands our vision and frees us from material and practical constraints. That tiny bonfire set by microbes inside the terrarium will gradually consume the available oxygen and generate CO_2 inside. Accumulated CO_2 and heat from the bonfire will gradually terminate the sustainability of the terrarium and eventually snuff out all life inside. That's what we humans are doing to the only Earth we are bestowed with.

Let's re-imagine one last time. This time, let us visualize another hypothetical scenario where the microbes living inside this small man-made terrarium got hold of a small solar panel and set it up inside the terrarium—to light a small LED bulb inside it. This is also a fictional visualization. Solar energy is now captured by the solar panel located inside the terrarium, and that energy is transferred to light up the LED bulb inside. Earlier, the sunlight that was falling upon the terrarium was partly absorbed by leaves and soil and partly reflected out and away. Absorbed sunlight inside was further partly converted to mass and partly remained as heat energy. Now, that equilibrium has changed because the solar panel inside the terrarium is capturing nearly all the sunlight that was earlier getting reflected away. Energy absorption inside the terrarium has increased due to the solar panel, causing increased heat retention and, hence, warming inside the terrarium.

One might already have an inkling of where this is headed.

By generating or capturing heat inside our terrarium Earth, we are transforming it into a potboiler that's getting heated from the sun outside, and we generate heat inside by burning fuel ourselves—to fund our lifestyles.

So far, we've been burning dirty fuel; now, we are striving to burn clean fuel instead.

Whether with clean or dirty fuel, we'll boil ourselves either way… all inside our terrarium Earth.

Instead of worrying about reducing our multiplying heat generation, the world has focused all its worries only on the fact that the heat we generate is not getting dissipated as fast as it used to—because greenhouse gases are shielding that heat dissipation. So, all current efforts are solely to reduce greenhouse gases in the atmosphere, while hardly anyone talks about reducing heat energy consumption, except as an exception in a footnote. All countries continue to strive to enhance their national per capita energy consumption because that's an indicator of economic activity and economic prosperity while blaming greenhouse gases for the resulting global warming.

The narrative as propagated is as it's heard—that burning fossil fuels causes global warming, and hence, the world should shift to renewable energy. This narrative is not incorrect but only partly correct. This partly correct narrative is propagated because it serves everyone—community, industry, politics, and business interests. I don't believe that the innumerable bright scientific minds are unaware of where the real problem lies and that heat addition is a much bigger devil than the greenhouse gas menace. So, one may wonder if it's deliberate not to attempt targeting the elephant in the room—the wasteful heat addition through human activities. There are already enough indications that the current partly correct narrative, to just shift to renewable energy, is not sufficient to reverse global warming. The impact of global warming is seen all around the human vicinity. The year 2023 was the hottest year ever on record. Let's further understand why the shift to renewable energy is a "partly" correct approach.

When fossil fuels are burned, they release energy and emissions. Everyone knows.

Emissions are rich in CO_2—a greenhouse gas that traps incoming sunlight by not allowing it to reflect back out of Earth's atmosphere—leading to global warming. So, the world is trying to shift to cleaner fuels that do not release CO_2. The world is encouraging and incentivizing the installation of cleaner sources of energy generation. COP28, the 28th meeting of the UN Climate Control body, resolved to limit global temperature rise by transitioning away from fossil fuels, tripling renewable energy, and tripling nuclear energy capacity. On the one hand, the world is moving on the path to curb greenhouse gas generation, while on the other hand, the world is actually *amplifying* heat energy generation within our ecosystem. As the newer nuclear plants and renewable energy plants get installed, is the fossil fuel-based power generation being dismantled? I think not, as that's tantamount to economic hara-kiri. Newer nuclear plants and renewable energy plants will become additive to the current fossil fuel-based power generation units—and it will only be in arithmetic percentage terms that countries will show their fossil fuel-based power has reduced. The intent is right; the outcome would perhaps not be.

The volume of our Earth's atmosphere, which dissipates heat out of our ecosystem, is limited. Our heat dissipation sink is limited. Imagine Earth as a ball contained within an atmosphere that is a bigger ball, and the outer surface of that bigger atmosphere ball is limited by its size and hence can dissipate only as much heat into space. As we increase the heat energy generation inside our ecosystem, we are bound to increase the heat resident within our ecosystem.

So, even if the world shifts to clean fuels instead of dirty fuels, we still arrive at the same conclusion—we'll continue to heat ourselves up with clean fuels instead of dirty fuels. Currently, the world is reducing 'emissions' while galloping unabated with enhanced energy consumption. What the right-hand giveth, the left hand taketh away. This contradiction is a self-fulfilling prophecy of inevitable doom.

Our pursuits toward cleaner energy need to be supplemented by cutting down energy consumption per se rather than targeting only energy-related emissions. The need of the hour is to address the root cause... the source... the genesis of the issue, and that is our wasteful energy usage. To be successful in our efforts to prevent further global temperature rise, the current strategy needs to be changed to a dual-pronged strategy—curbing emissions plus reducing energy usage per se.

Energy

'Reduction in energy usage' does not resonate with the business interests of communities because it tends to get equated to 'De-Growth'. Justifiably, the world does not want 'de-growth' because the prime mover decisions in the world are taken by people in power bolstered by industry and finance. People need jobs, and de-growth would take away those jobs; nobody can live with that… understandably so. De-growth would lead to a reduction in business activity, and it's the businesses that fund the money to run this world and put money in people's pockets to buy stuff for survival. Everyone wants economic progress; nobody wants 'de-growth!' That's an understandable and appreciated fact of life. 'Reduction in energy usage' may be a boon for human survival, but a bane for business activity and jobs. Which government in their right minds can propose to take up a path leading to reduced jobs? None whatsoever.

For that reason, our efforts to reduce energy consumption need to be such that do not lead to 'De-Growth' and do not lead to job loss. Only such initiatives would be worthy of consideration as only such initiatives would be publicly acceptable. 'Reduction in energy usage' needs to be targeted in a way that it becomes practically acceptable. That's easier said than done. We need to start searching for avenues for 'Reduction in energy usage' in a politically and socially acceptable manner, in the same earnest way we apply ourselves toward our pursuit for reduction in emissions.

Looking at it from both perspectives, the approach needs rationalization and calibration.

With this spirit, let's try to exemplify here how we can selectively pursue 'Reduction in energy usage' in a humane manner sensitive to business and jobs too.

The only unscheduled global temperature reduction was between 1492 and 1600 CE. Then, the global temperature had dropped by 0.15 degrees Celsius, and the CO_2 had reduced by 7-10 ppm. The cause for this unscheduled global temperature reduction is attributed to the tragic large-scale depopulation of the Americas after European contact[12]. Approximately 56 million people perished due to the imported diseases that natives were not immune to, resulting in the non-use of agricultural land. This is one solid actual proof that the decline in population reversed the global temperature rise. The role of population in global warming is not something novel, but rather logical. The more people on the planet, the more is the total energy consumption by the increased number of people on the globe. This is not something that's incomprehensible, but rather evidently perceptible. As evident as it might be, has anyone ever heard any Climate Control body saying, "Let's consider population control to rein in global temperature?"

Instance of population reduction in 1492 - 1600 CE leading to reduced global temperature was brought in because that is a historical proof to bolster our case. Is there any other non-cyclical period of global temperature reduction that mankind has known in the near past... none whatsoever. This one instance we know of in 1492 - 1600 CE provides the sanctity to our case. We must take cue from this historical proof of 1492 - 1600 CE and should consider adding 'population control' within our basket of climate reversal strategies. If we believe, as we surely do, that humans caused the current spike in global warming through human activities, then it would be plain & simple to reduce the pace at which we keep adding humans on this planet. 'Population control' should not remain just a social factor, rather it needs to be nurtured and incentivized as a prominent tool to combat global warming. Reduction in population growth rates needs to be incentivized at community level as well as national & global levels, as this is a proven logical path that has a historical proof of being effective. 'Population control' as a climate combat tool would not be economically disruptive - as was our concern when we started this discourse. India and China being the most populous countries in the world should obviously be the flag bearers of 'Population control' as a climate combat tool, reaping benefits not only through climate-related incentives but also associated benefits like reduced stress on resources & jobs. Imagine nations earning carbon credits by reducing the population growth rate!

'Population control' is a socially sensitive subject, hence the apprehension of reprisals, which results in not many takers in the policy formulation circles, especially of Indian polity. By fate or by design, any efforts in this direction, especially in India, are perceived to be targeted toward a particular community.

But in the global interest and in the interest of survivability, the proposition of 'Population control' as a climate combat tool may well find the requisite support it deserves to drive the momentum thereafter. This is the single most important climate initiative that deserves attention, but never came to be brought up by any nation thus far.

Talking about the 'basket of climate reversal strategies', let's try filling this basket with a few more novel strategies.

How would it sound if it were proposed that the relooking at buildings would yield much more beneficial results to combat climate change compared to automotive emissions! In light of our predilection toward electric vehicles being the harbinger to address climate change, it may sound bizarre to talk of buildings in the same breath. Buildings - Residential Housing as well as commercial buildings, are never on our radar when we talk climate reversal for obvious reasons... how can buildings lead to climate change… is the mindset. Actually, it would be shocking to know that the energy consumption & emissions from Residential and Commercial buildings rank at the top of the table - accounting for a huge 17.5% of all emissions [13]. Emissions (and hence the energy) from road transport come a distant second at only 11.9%. Yet, our prime attention remains toward decarbonizing through the use of renewable fuels or electric vehicles in the automobile sector. This is not to say that the aspect has gone unnoticed. COP28 (UN Climate Change Conference) does recognize the building sector and its contribution to climate change and has proposed to focus on sustainable cooling by using nature-based cooling, increased efficiency of cooling, and phasedown of refrigerants & air-conditioning to reduce emissions. But there's hardly any visible action on the ground related to this aspect. How can it be possible to do 'nature-based cooling' of the tall building complexes that continue to sprout all around in everyone's vicinity? The world continues to install glass facade office complexes with impunity, knowing fully well that air-conditioning needs of glass buildings are huge energy guzzlers compared to ordinary brick buildings[14]. The world continues to replace our conventional windows with glass doors because they are in vogue – only to shade them away later most of the time to protect privacy and switch on the air-con to get rid of the heat the glass allows in. Addressing the manner in which we build our buildings and develop our cities is as essential a tool to combat climate change as anything else.

If one happens to stroll into one of the old residences like *havelis* of a bygone era, in any of the old cities anywhere in the world, one will experience that the buildings are much cooler inside without any air-conditioning. That's because old buildings were constructed primarily of thick brick walls and did not use any glass. Glass facades retain the heat within the buildings, as the greenhouse effect is. Even where a minimum amount of glass was used in earlier days, the glass was painted. The use of natural ventilation used to be the key feature to keep them cool in earlier building constructions. All in all, old buildings were constructed with the mindset to keep them cool inside even in the hot sun. But our new buildings are constructed with every other objective except to naturally cool their insides. New building construction is driven by commercial needs – to fit in maximum working space within the limited plot space and of course driven by aesthetics and to reduce construction time. Glass construction has a glasshouse effect – it retains heat within. First, we make office spaces as glasshouses – with the argument that it'll bring natural light in. Then we realize that the sunlight causes glares on eyes and on computer screens. Eventually & invariably all such glasshouse buildings are shielded by blinds during daytime. The outcome is the need to keep the air-conditioning running all the time to cool these buildings. Air-conditioning cools the buildings, but heats up the environment, and the air conditioner is only shifting the heat from inside to outside, while electricity consumed in running the air-con adds to the heating. Across the world, the growth rate of the air-conditioning industry is in double digits, we can well imagine the impact on global temperatures.

The need of the hour is to take a step back and prioritize 'nature-based cooling' for our buildings, as also recommended by COP28 (the UN Climate Change Conference). Lest we forget, energy consumption in buildings is much higher than even the cumulative emissions from road transport.

Apart from the 'nature-based cooling' advocated for buildings, there's another perspective in the context of buildings. Families are now becoming smaller and more nuclear – that's how life evolves with prosperity. While families are getting smaller, houses are getting bigger. It's natural that as affluence increases, so does an individual's propensity to switch to a bigger dwelling. While this is a universal phenomenon common across nations, the per person residential area is starkly high in the western counties. The bigger the house, the more energy in terms of air-conditioning it needs. Weather being extreme in western countries, air-conditioning costs are particularly high throughout the year.

Another aspect that adds to the energy consumption is the ceiling height. High ceilings are a norm in individual houses in western countries, thereby requiring more energy to keep them conditioned.

Again, in developed cold countries, it's common to use heating systems to heat the entire houses. Inhabitants of underdeveloped countries just put on more insulation to keep themselves warm, thereby consuming/generating less heat. In developed economies, it's common to use an electric dryer to dry the laundry. That's the way it is. Inhabitants of underdeveloped countries dry it out in the sun. Aren't these something like low-hanging fruits that would immediately cut down our fuel requirements?

Lifestyle changes like these would directly and immediately reduce fuel consumption and hence the heat generation. The effect is cumulative; per capita energy consumption is quite high in the west compared to that in the east. For instance, Canada's per capita energy consumption is 14 times higher than in India[15], to give perspective. That's not a subtle or incremental difference; rather, the magnitude of the increase is multifold!

So, when an individual emigrates from Asia to Canada, that individual effectively increases its energy consumption by 14 times! The same individual, when in Asia, was consuming much less energy and hence heating the world much less, compared to when the individual migrated to a western country… by a factor of 14 times! This is a very stark comparison and should be an eye-opener for the world to consider for long-term survival. With this realization, let us consider where it makes more sense for the world to grow its habitat… in the west or in the east?

Every year, millions of people migrate from Asia to colder countries like the USA and Canada, which have multiple times higher per capita energy consumption. To give a perspective, Indian immigration to Canada[21] has tripled since 2013 - from 32,828 in 2013 to 118,095 in 2022. Electricity consumption per capita[22] for Canada is 16,602 KWH versus only 1,297 KWH for India. That means migration from India to Canada increased the world's electricity consumption in just a single year, 2022, by a huge 1,810 Megawatts! The reduction of migration must be incorporated as a key tool within COP28 (UN Climate Change Conference) initiatives.

Business expansion in the west by importing manpower from the east serves contrary to the goals of reversing climate change. An example should be good to elucidate the point. Suppose a new manufacturing facility is to be set-up that will employ 2,000 persons. One option is for that facility to be set-up in a western country like Canada and import a part of the workforce from Asia to live in the west and supplement the local workforce. The other option is to locate that facility in the eastern country and import part of the workforce from the west to live in the east, to support the local workforce. Which option do you think is more environmentally friendly? In the first option, those 2,000 persons consume 14 times higher energy to live in the west, while the latter option lowers their energy consumption by 14 times. The lesser the energy consumption, the lesser the emissions as well, apart from the fact that it's the energy consumption per se that actually is the evil that heats up our planet – as already discussed in the preceding text.

Local businesses needs are obviously a priority, and every community in the west or the east needs local businesses to thrive. That's a given. The point here is that the macro-level picture for environmental sustainability requires the world to adopt much more than just the current approach of emission reduction. Multi-pronged novel approaches are the need of the hour if the world really wants to be able to slow down the current trend of global warming, if not achieve climate reversal.

Population growth, people migration to the west, building construction, and business expansion in the west... all these aspects need to be accounted for within the UN Climate rectification protocols, with due incentives for these to be successful. Asian countries, in particular, have missed out on noticing the importance of such parameters and thereby missed out on requiring these parameters to be included within the UN Climate Change framework.

Where we come to with this argument is that the human migration to western countries is a significant factor toward increasing the per capita energy consumption, and hence this needs to be discouraged entirely. Shifting the population to countries with harsher climates is environmentally unfriendly and unsustainable. Per capita energy consumption needs to be a prominent factor to be included within the parameters with which the UN Climate Change body sets a corrective path for various countries to follow for climate reversal. Take the recent COP28 (UN Climate Change Conference), for example, where several laudable initiatives have been set for countries to follow, but there has been absolutely ZERO mention regarding the need for the world to rationalize its per capita energy consumption.

Solar

Every year, Gigawatts of solar panels are installed inside our terrarium Earth atmosphere. That's because solar energy is perceived to be the savior that would free our world from the perils of dirty energy derived from fossil fuels. Millions of solar panels already have patched the Earth's surface, and more are being added continuously. As we read this book, newer supply chains are getting created to cater to the insatiable demand for solar panels. More & more of our deserts and rooftops will keep getting covered with solar panels. Solar energy is clean, so let's maximize it… that's the new-age paradigm and hence the focus area is to harness solar power.

The issue is that solar panels are designed to reflect as little as possible. They are akin to black bodies. When sunlight falls upon the solar panels, generally, 90-95% of it gets captured by the solar panel, depending on the angle of incidence of sunrays. Out of this 90-95% of captured and absorbed solar energy, only a small 20-25% gets converted into electricity, and the remaining 70-75% gets converted to heat that goes on to eventually heat up the atmosphere in the vicinity. A major part of the sunrays that were previously getting bounced & radiated away from the desert surface gets captured by solar panels, and that captured heat energy heats up the environment through local convective currents.

In effect, we are trapping more and more solar energy by using solar panels and ultimately converting it partly into electricity and largely into heat. Solar energy that would have earlier bounced off the Earth's surface now gets captured in the solar panels and becomes resident within the chamber that our Earth's atmosphere is. Undoubtedly, solar energy is clean as it does not add greenhouse gases, but it adds a bigger devil by itself by capturing more 'heat' into our atmosphere. Heat that would have got reflected back and out is becoming more resident within all around us.

Shifting from fossil fuels to solar power is beneficial for emission reduction, but the fact remains that solar power also enhances heat retention within our atmosphere!

Deserts particularly have a role to play in that they reflect away most of the incoming solar radiation and prevent the Earth's surface from getting hotter. Deserts do not bind the heat onto the Earth's surface; that's the reason deserts become cold… freezing cold… as soon as the sun goes down.

On the contrary, solar panels are designed to absorb the maximum sunlight that falls on them. Hence, they do quite the opposite of what deserts do. When we cover our deserts with solar panels, we are 100% reversing the function of deserts – from being reflectors to becoming heat absorbers. The absorbed heat remains inside our Earth's atmosphere, gradually heating it up more and more every day. This is something that the world has not woken up to yet.

Solar energy is undoubtedly clean, as it does not add carbon to the atmosphere. But it does enhance heat addition to our atmosphere, and that's the real issue at hand – global warming.

While on Solar, it would be worthwhile to also clarify a misnomer. Solar is the primary source of all other forms of energy. All forms of energy – dirty or clean – renewable or non-renewable – they all originate from the sun. But only renewable energy is called sustainable. Why? Why aren't the fossil fuels like petrol & diesel renewable?

'Renewable' terminology is actually a misnomer. Every form of energy is renewable – be it solar, wind, tidal, biomass, nuclear, or our so tainted gasoline & diesel. The source of all these forms of energy is single – the SUN. Wind energy comes from the winds that are generated due to the temperature differentials between various landmasses & oceans – and that differential heating is caused by the SUN. Tidal energy comes from the upliftment of sea levels – that upliftment being caused by the gravitational pull of the moon that is held in place due to the gravitational forces between the Earth and the SUN. Hydro power comes because of the rain cycle and precipitation caused due to the SUN. Plants grow because of sunlight and form the biomass that we are now converting into energy. Petrol & diesel come from the oil that came from the biomass that was formed millions of years ago and got decomposed to form oil. Everything comes from the SUN. All forms of energy are actually renewable, just that the time taken to renew them varies from a couple of seconds to millions of years. We loosely refer to some forms of energy as renewable – because these renewable energies get 'replenished' much faster compared to other forms.

Nuclear

Nuclear energy is clean because it does not generate CO_2. Atoms are split using nuclear reactors to liberate the heat that was erstwhile resident inside the atoms. The amount of heat that the atoms hold between them is colossal, and all this heat, after getting liberated from their atoms, hugely adds to the Earth's atmosphere. Nuclear activity is clean from an emissions perspective but ends up releasing the heat that was bound inside the atoms.

Paradoxically, among other initiatives, COP28 (UN Climate Change Conference) primarily proposes to limit the rise in global temperatures by transitioning away from fossil fuels and by replacing our energy requirements with renewable energy generation systems. *Tripling* the nuclear energy is one key method proposed to achieve this objective. In the light of all that we have discussed just now, evaluate this initiative and judge. This initiative, as per COP28, requires replacing the energy from fossil fuels by installing new nuclear plants. This initiative encourages adding more energy generation facilities, and that's where the world is unmindfully headed – to add more & more energy generation facilities. Our aim to curb 'emissions' is actually amplifying energy generation within our ecosystem.

What nuclear facilities achieve is to unlock and release the humungous energy that was erstwhile locked inside the atoms, manifesting itself as heat that adds to our already heated planet. This unlocked energy is used to generate electricity, and that electricity also ultimately converts into heat somewhere down the line where electricity is utilized. All the energy generated during the nuclear process ultimately manifests itself in terms of heat that adds to our already heated planet.

Travel

As human prosperity increases, so does the propensity for leisure travel. What good is the wealth if it does not expand one's reach to further-off destinations? The primary travel choice for most people, if they can afford it, would be to fly off as far as possible. In this context, consider this… a single long-haul flight between, say, Frankfurt and Singapore consumes a mammoth 100 tons of aviation fuel! If that doesn't ring a bell, consider this: Taking 550 persons flying on that plane, each person consumes fuel more than double their own body weight on this travel route.

Air travel is extremely energy-intensive. We've already understood through the preceding text that it's the 'energy consumption' that's the root of climate change; of course, emissions make it worse. To rein in the energy consumption, air travel needs to be another target of our attention. Undoubtedly, air travel generates employment and is the breadwinner for a large percentage of the population. This industry needs to survive simply due to its business and social obligations. At the same time, this industry needs rationalization to reduce its energy consumption.

A possibility in the context could be to moderate the growth in long-distance air travel. Surely, there would be abundant places of beauty in one's vicinity that are generally ignored in preference to going off to far-off places like, say, Reykjavík in Iceland. Local travel should be encouraged not just in the country's own economic & social interest, but rather as an essential tool toward saving the planet and climate reversal. Local travel versus long-distance travel needs to be incentivized and factored in within our basket of climate reversal strategies. Reducing long-distance air travel for business purposes also needs rationalization - it would also improve business's bottom line apart from the benevolent contribution in reducing heating up of the planet. We have all learned in the COVID times that business travel is avoidable. Businesses of the day are now equipped with necessary IT infrastructure to be used to prevent air travel. Meetings that earlier were not possible to be conducted remotely can well be done now online. Cutting down on air travel needs to be prioritized among the business sector and could well be incentivized with the ultimate aim being to reduce our planet's energy consumption.

Mass transport modes for public transport are way more energy-efficient compared to the usage of individual cars. In terms of energy consumed per person per kilometer, trains are 4 times more energy-efficient compared to cars. When inefficiency due to traffic congestion on roads is added to this, the efficiency of mass transport modes gets even better. Considering this, significant infrastructural developments are needed particularly in cities to create a web of metro rail lines and for high-speed inter-city rail travel. Target the metro rail as the default mode of travel for all classes of people... particularly office-goers. The transition to electric cars and hydrogen transport is already underway in the right direction. The generation of necessary infrastructure for mass transport would also generate jobs.

Biofuels

The world is going lock, stock, and barrel to grow plants as biomass - to convert them to 'clean' oil so that this clean oil can then be burned to generate clean energy. Significant investment is currently flowing into projects that convert biomass into biofuels. These biofuels are similar to gasoline (petrol) & diesel as we know, except that they are generated from biomass like corn, sugarcane molasses, plant residue & the like. When such biofuels are used in the aviation industry, these are called Sustainable Aviation Fuels (SAF). The biofuels and SAF industry are the fast-rising trend because these are largely carbon neutral, i.e., carbon dioxide picked by plants during growing is released back into the atmosphere during the burning of these biofuels. From that perspective, biofuels should indeed be our preferred path toward renewable energy.

But the relatively unpublicized fact is also that growing plants need fertilizers, whereas the world is fast running out of its limited phosphatic fertilizer reserves. Some research[16] says that the world may run out of phosphatic fertilizers much earlier than we run out of energy. No phosphatic fertilizer means no crop cultivation. The assessment is that phosphatic rock will last only the next 300 years or so at current usage[17] – that figure may reduce drastically if the limited phosphatic fertilizer supply is diverted to biofuels as well.

Before plunging headlong into mass production of biofuels, the world needs to assess its impact on associated resources like farmland utilization, and in particular, the impact on the limited supply of phosphatic fertilizer.

Phosphatic fertilizer is going to run out earlier than fuel, so developing alternatives should be a priority. In current agricultural practices, only 8% of phosphatic fertilizer is taken up by plants[18], while the remaining 92% leaches into the lower soil and goes to waste. Wider adoption of hydroponics will help, as it allows full utilization of applied phosphates compared to just 8% utilization in conventional growing.

New forms of clean energy like biofuels, solar, and other renewables are like a double-edged sword – they provide clean energy while heating us up. Whether it's energy from biofuels or fossil fuels, all end up heating our biosphere – this aspect is not thought of currently in climate circles. A cleaner path to heat ourselves eventually causes only heating. Energy from fossil fuels is also actually solar energy that was trapped naturally and has been lying trapped for millions of years. Biofuels follow the same route - except that biofuels get harvested in a much smaller time frame of over a few months. Heat addition by biofuels is the same as by conventional fossil fuels. Switching to biofuels is better than consuming fossil fuels in terms of emission reduction, but it's equally impactful in terms of heat/energy addition to the atmosphere, and its impact on the limited phosphatic fertilizer supply is something that needs careful vigilance.

Dietary Habits

The world's rice consumption is increasing year on year. Rice cultivation consumes significantly more water compared to millets that grow easily in a dry climate. This is generally known.

But a lesser-known fact is that rice cultivation releases enormous methane into the atmosphere[19]. Globally, around 8% of agricultural greenhouse gas emissions are produced by growing rice. Methane is a far more deadly greenhouse gas compared to CO_2, by a factor of 84 on a twenty-year timeframe! This means that as the world keeps increasing its rice consumption, so will the methane emissions also multiply. Directionally, every percentage increase in rice consumption will proportionately increase the methane release into the atmosphere, and that methane gas is 84 times more potent greenhouse gas compared to CO_2.

On the other hand, millets thrive in much less water, even in dry weather, and do not release as much methane. But the world's consumption of millets is reducing, while rice consumption is increasing.

Overall impact is an increase in methane gas emissions – a very powerful greenhouse gas.

Switching dietary habits from rice to wheat and millets would help reduce global warming, as that will reduce methane emissions from rice fields. Reduction in stubble burning would come as an added benefit. One may wonder why India does not quantify its recent push toward a millet economy in these terms and get it captured within the climate rectification protocol and claim its benefits.

Everyone knows non-vegetarian food is more energy-intensive, but little do we realize that livestock emissions also account for nearly 32 per cent of human-caused methane emissions.

Our mindset needs a directional rectification to consume less energy rather than anything else.

The food we consume should be driven by whatever took less energy to produce it. Animal foods take significantly more energy to produce compared to plant foods. Without stigmatizing any particular line of foods, all that is submitted here is that food choices are a significant contributor to energy consumption. It would do well to consider Energy Intensity Indices for every processed food that we produce and consume to offer direction to the general populace, just like the nutritional labels are printed on food packaging.

Chemical Energy

Talk about chemical energy release. Detonations in war are all chemical energy releases from gunpowder. All the wars that perpetually go on in some part of the world add hugely to the heating of our atmosphere. Every weapon that's fired adds to heat us up. In this context, shouldn't the weapon manufacturing industry be climate taxed by bringing it under the ambit of the Climate Control body? We haven't yet heard of any country taking this line of approach when contributing their thoughts in the annual body meetings called the Conference of the Parties of the United Nations. Countries manufacturing and selling weapons need to be held accountable and taxed in this context. Weapon manufacture needs to be reduced or made so expensive that their use is curtailed, all embedded and penalized within the framework of our collective climate control actions.

Fireworks for celebrations are something that bring collective joy but need to introduce minimalism. This is the paradox of plenty. I have plenty of firecrackers, so my neighbor must outdo me, or vice versa. Humans have an inherent propensity & desire of standing out by exhibiting their surplus. That is achieved by doing more of what the other person is doing, to flaunt through excess. Wonder, why does one need those endless strings of sequential firecrackers that a person lights and goes away to smoke, while those firecracker strings go on & on by themselves for eternity – causing all kinds of inconvenience to others while adding colossal heat to our atmosphere. Firecracker production needs to be selectively harnessed by prohibiting sequential type varieties, and allowing only the ones where a person has to put in effort for every single one of it to be lighted – so the gentleman gets exhausted and goes away to sleep sooner.

Bigger Homes, Bigger Cars, Bigger TVs, Bigger Travel – all driven by human desire to flaunt! Having deep pockets should not earn us the right to heat the one collective globe we have. Such energy guzzlers have to be severely discouraged, for mankind to see more days. An electric car still consumes & adds heat. Airplanes running on biofuels still generate the same heat as conventional planes do. Burning petrol unlocks & adds heat that was captured a million years ago in oil, while biofuel adds the same heat by capturing it more recently. That's the only difference. Choices of Work-from-Home or Work-from-Office need to be dictated and regulated by what consumes less energy rather than anything else. Our choices of travel need to be looked at through a climate lens. Actually, as the end user, every single individual should look at everything we consume through an 'energy' lens and choose options that consume less energy.

Free Electricity… well, that's like shooting our own foot that's already immersed in a simmering pot. I yearn to see governmental regimes that ostracize consumption of energy rather than precipitating our already precarious situation by giving free electricity or by subsidizing fuel. A certain minimum subsidy for the impoverished class is undeniably an understandable social obligation, but beyond a limit, we need to tax ourselves heavily - to discourage wasteful consumption.

The world's focus needs a paradigm shift - to be 'Energy Minimal'.

'Carbon neutral' will come automatically as a welcome and beneficial side-effect.

If the world applies itself in such a direction, there will be numerous other uncharted avenues for climate rectification waiting to be discovered by sharper minds. Don't get it wrong. Shifting from fossil fuels to clean fuels is the right path. But all forms of energy – dirty or clean – heat us up. The devil lies in wasteful energy consumption that needs to be curbed as a priority – by every individual.

We are all in the same pot, even if we're boiling it with cleaner energy. The pot is simmering and will eventually boil over – that's inevitable. That's the nature of the beast. We can't beat it, but we can prolong the time if we take the right decisions now.

We need to retract and move away from energy consumerism toward energy minimalism.

That's unhesitatingly beneficial for survival... err... for prolonging survival.

The impact of global warming is being experienced in real-time and fast; there's no room for denial anymore. The impact on the food chain would be severe. The world's climate initiatives, aimed at preventing a temperature increase beyond 1.5 degrees Celsius compared to pre-industrial levels, have fallen flat. In March 2024, the world had already surpassed that threshold.

It's now critical that the world's focus should expand toward reducing energy consumption per se, and efforts need to be made in this direction to seek energy reduction avenues that create alternative industry to minimize impact on the livelihood of people. A broader perspective is needed by reducing 'heat addition' to the atmosphere, rather than a narrow-minded obsession with lowering emissions only.

At an individual level, everyone must carry their 'energy' lens at all times.

Phew! We'll conclude the climate discussion now.

Getting a grasp on things that should matter the most for survival deems to be an accomplishment deserving a congratulatory drink! Getting thus far on the climate subject means you have the penchant for venturing beyond the ordinary discourse and engaging in meaningful discussion that can cause a discernible change. Relative esoteric concepts on climate were elucidated though in brief, but hopefully sufficiently lucid for absorption by yourself. As would hence be perceptible, it's imperative to take the climate discourse further through engaging with the right audience that can influence and shape alternative decision-making. It's deeply encouraged but remains the reader's prerogative to indulge in expansive dissemination of this knowledge so gained among the people around, for the expansion of climate awareness and possible course correction in times to come. It's deeply encouraged that you share this knowledge so that you become the cause... the harbinger... of the change that you want to see in your world. Small steps can lead to big changes.

Reality is that this wish may be a chimera. The world will continue to run as it currently is, and the climate will keep getting harsher. So, we'll do the next best thing – to take advantage of climate change by focusing & practicing hydroponics. As the weather gets harsher, hydroponics' profitability will continue to rise – thereby creating a future-proof & very lucrative business opportunity.

Chapter 2

Why Hydroponics

How many professions can one think of where payback can be as little as a year? Meaning the investment returns in a year or so, without having to spend years learning it, without the need for skilled manpower, without the need to own vast expanses of land, without the need for bureaucratic licensing hurdles, scalable to any extent, pesticide-free, with multiple times faster growth compared to - how many come to your mind? And how many would be such where profitability improves in the future, as the climate gets harsher all around us?

Hydroponics is the practice of profusely growing exotic vegetables at any scale – commercial or hobby - without soil – at an accelerated growth rate – 3 to 5 times faster growth. Pesticide-free. Vast fields as in agriculture – not needed. Can be done in available space – indoor or outdoor. Hydroponics is free of climate vagaries; it's certain. It's weather-independent, can be done any time of year. Want to grow strawberries in hot climates… sure. And the hydroponic produce fetches much higher prices compared to its soil-grown brethren because it's better looking and bigger sized. It's a money spinner!

Wait.

If it's so good and lucrative, why haven't I seen it happening all around me?

Logical question.

We did mention early on in the book about Ashwin Sawant, who is an entrepreneur in Pune and became a hydroponic millionaire through growing fodder. And another millionaire, Vivek Raj Poojary, who featured in Forbes India for his pioneering indoor hydroponic farms growing saffron and medicinal plants. There are many more who are doing it profitably in India, while remaining out of the news… of course, as hydroponics is not in the limelight yet.

There is already tremendous growth happening in hydroponic ventures worldwide – especially in the USA & Europe. It's slow in India yet because of a genuine knowledge availability issue. The USA & Europe are research-driven knowledge economies where they apply the right know-how to do hydroponics – supplemented by capital & technology deployment. In India, hydroponic information is learned in bits and pieces by individuals – mostly through online free information, put together by further cutting corners. Knowledge deficit leads to sub-optimal results. Free online information has a purpose – to generate clicks – that can help advertisements to land on that page – that's their revenue source. Free or cheaply priced online information is grossly inadequate – providing just surface information. Mostly, equipment suppliers of hydroponics profit by just selling their equipment – install and go away, leaving the buyer stranded with an assemblage of pipes and fittings sitting on behemoth structures.

Hydroponics is an extremely profitable commercial venture if done right, and the book tells how to do it just right. Hydroponics is increasingly being practiced since long - more so in the current situation when the climate is worsening. Case studies are presented in the commercial section of the hydroponics chapter, where the costing and revenue details will be provided for some variations of hydroponic ventures – that will show the variation in payback as one opts for different designs & configurations. Payback periods vary depending on the choices you make – from an enviable one year to 3 years. This means if one is to invest X amount of capital today, hydroponics has the potential to return that X amount within a year or more, depending upon the configuration. Actually, 7 commercial configurations with their costing are presented in the commercial section, wherein the impact on profitability, i.e., payback, is exhibited. It's early in the book to explain these here, without having the awareness regarding the component aspects – which comes subsequently & gradually in the book. For now, it'll suffice to say that these case studies exemplify why it's important to be aware of the impact parameters that directly impact profitability. These case studies allow the reader to make factually knowledgeable choices in line with one's funding, appetite and vision. Choices one makes impact the future life – in business as in personal lives. Choices should be made carefully - with all due considerations. In the sphere of hydroponics at least, this book provides you with the necessary tools to make informed choices… decisions. There are things about hydroponics that are never revealed, but here they are.

This book provides the entire 100% factual hydroponic knowledge – all practical and in mostly non-technical language. All pitfalls and all success factors. Without compromising on knowledge content, deliberately, the level of technicality has been reduced in this book - for easy understanding and a fun reading - to maintain a novel-like reading experience. Several aspects that have hitherto remained hidden even to professional hydroponics – deliberately or by ignorance - are also brought out in the open in this book. This book would enable the reader to practice hydroponics profitably at a commercial scale or enjoyably as a hobby to start.

——•••——

61

Now, what has climate got to do with hydroponics?

Why and how are climate change and hydroponics connected?

We already have situations around us wherein yields of some types of crops have started reducing due to climate change. Crops need a certain range of ambient temperatures to survive. How will they survive in searing hot air – scorching them? It's not something that's probable, rather something that's ongoing, with increasing intensity as every other day progresses. We are already witnessing reduced yields of olive & coffee plantations; saffron production is becoming dearer and the like. Various studies have established that the vegetable yields in open field cultivation are being impacted, some even predicting that open field cultivation of some vegetables like tomatoes might become unsustainable in the future. Due to human temerity, CO_2 & temperature levels have far exceeded all previously known CO_2 levels that were even at the peaks of earlier extinctions.

Growing vegetables in artificially controlled environments is already a trend in western countries. Many countries have already resorted to this. The transition is already underway in a big way. Ongoing climate change is what makes hydroponic ventures more profitable, and that equation will only keep improving with time – as climate change increases, so will the hydroponic profitability.

Hydroponic crop production has experienced exponential growth throughout the world. In Europe, the Netherlands is contributing the highest market share in the global hydroponics market. The Netherlands also has the maximum area covered by greenhouse farms – where hydroponics is practiced inside a controlled environment – immune to the vagaries of climate change and produces all kinds of vegetables like cucumbers, tomatoes, carrots, paprika, lettuce, spinach, etc. The average utilized agricultural area per greenhouse horticulture farm in the Netherlands more than doubled from 2007 to 2021. In 2007, the average farmland per greenhouse horticulture farm in the Netherlands was 2.6 hectares. By 2021, this average had increased to 6.1 hectares[20].

Spain produces tons of greenhouse vegetables and fruits like tomatoes, peppers, zucchinis, cucumbers, strawberries, etc., using hydroponic techniques and is growing rapidly. The land area used for greenhouse cultivation in the country has grown at a rapid rate in recent years. A similar story unfolds in France, Germany, and other European cities.

Globally, North America ranks at the top when it comes to hydroponics produce, with Europe second. Asia-Pacific comes third in the adoption of hydroponic systems worldwide, especially in China, Australia, and South Korea. Rapid urbanization is a key factor that induces people to adopt new agricultural methods close to where they live, to get hands-on the fresh produce. Globally, the most popular plants currently grown hydroponically are tomatoes, lettuce, leafy vegetables, cucumber, pepper, strawberry, and herbs – grown in abundance.

Hydroponics is being practiced on the ground (and also in space) and growing rapidly worldwide. Hydroponics is no longer a connoisseur's choice; it has become popular among the masses of late. Hydroponic growth is rapid, being taken up commercially and on rooftops as an alternative horticulture.

Hydroponics as a business venture is very profitable when practiced correctly, and profitability would keep increasing as the weather gets harsher. Doing it correctly is the key, for which practical knowledge is needed – this book provides. This is an activity that can be scaled up gradually and incrementally. This is an activity that does not require a person to own vast farmlands and can be practiced in any available free space – even rooftops or basements. A person does not need years of field experience to practice hydroponics, meaning a person need not be a farmer. Hydroponic cultivation needs much less water compared to traditional cultivation – just one-tenth in some configurations. Hydroponics does not involve extreme labor as in conventional agriculture; rather, it is fun while being financially rewarding at the same time. Hydroponics does not involve a steep learning curve. After reading through this book properly, you can really start off like an expert.

Even if the reader does not want to pursue commercial hydroponics, home horticulture would certainly be of interest. Home gardening is generally close to the heart of most people. Profusely growing vegetables & flowering plants, fast and easy, within the confines of one's home remains a dream almost every city dweller cherishes. The bliss of seeing the fast growth in plants that one has sown by oneself has immense therapeutic impact. This growth, when multiplied through hydroponic techniques, becomes visible on a daily basis, and the bliss becomes ecstatic!

The hydroponic expertise in this book is structured for the reader to practice both – commercial and hobby level – getting more profitable as the weather conditions get harsher. All concepts will remain the same, future-proof.

There has to be a reason for everything.

You have chanced upon this book for a reason that life may have presented as an opportunity. Does the environment have a role to play? This will be discussed in the end through real and unbelievable scientific experiments.

This book will impart all the hydroponic information – mostly practical and also some theoretical – that will allow the reader to embark upon a life-transformative journey of lucratively growing veggies without soil – a very profitable commercial venture, or just as a rewarding hobby. This book allows one to become a hobby practitioner of hydroponics as well as to initiate a professional journey toward commercial hydroponics. It empowers the reader to pursue hydroponics as a secondary, or primary occupation, or to just indulge in an extraordinary way of a greenful life – either way getting future-ready from a climate perspective.

The hydroponic expertise is narrated more like a novel, rather than a manual, to keep it interesting and largely non-technical.

——◆◆——

Chapter 3

The Hydroponic Path

Nature encompasses the very essence of our world—the intricate tapestry of existence that weaves together the physical, the living, and the cosmic. It encompasses the laws, elements, and phenomena of the physical world, including life itself. Nature refers to everything in the physical world that exists independently of human creation. It includes plants, animals, mountains, oceans, stars, and more—elements shaped by natural forces and processes. These are the aspects of our world that persist despite human intervention, such as wild animals, forests, and rocks.

Everyone has a different perspective when it comes to nature. Greens... expansive forests alive with lush verdant greens. Greens have been the cornerstone for civilizations to commence & thrive. Humans settle where greens exist or where greens can happen, with greens forming the basis of sustenance for all terrestrial life forms to exist. All aquatic life forms also can trace their origin one way or another to vegetative forms - like plankton that fill our oceans.

For some reasons, greens are said to have a calming effect on humans. Be it Feng Shui or Vaastu or a cornucopia of free online advice, everyone recommends bringing home some greens. Green is a color associated with health, vigor, and soundness of body and mind. Green pervades our existence in myriad forms to convey that it's okay... like a green traffic light that says it's okay to go on.

But plants loathe green. Plants don't like the color green!

Bizarre as it may sound, facts can sometimes seem so contrary to obvious logic that makes them unbelievable. But facts are facts. Plants grow where sunlight is – a universal truth. But do the plants need all the sunlight? Do the plants absorb all the sunlight that falls upon them? Sunlight comprises a spectrum of different wavelengths from red to violet – that everyone knows as VIBGYOR, and that's just the visible spectrum. What plants pick up is only what they need from the complete bandwidth of light wavelengths that fall upon them. And plants do *not* pick up the green wavelength much. They rather reflect away the green wavelengths – and when those rejected green wavelengths get captured by human eyes, we perceive the plants as green. That's how life is - one's reject becomes another's bliss.

In the context of what this book tries to address, where do the greens grow? Soil would probably come foremost. Practically every aspect of nature contributes to green growth. To avoid an extended discussion on the subject that's already well known, requirements for plants to grow naturally would be simplified to soil, water, air, and light. With these 4 basics being available, seeds will sprout into plants naturally.

Where does hydroponics come in?

Natural growth has limitations. Plants will grow only as allowed by the availability of nutrients in the soil, or as allowed by the availability of sunlight, not to mention the occasional toxic components like arsenic and lead that might be present in the soil and may get picked up by plants. Almost all the pests that plague plant growth also originate from the soil.

What if the nutrition provided by soil can be mimicked and vastly improved in an alternative medium? What if the light is made available to plants not just for a few hours, but for extended periods of time? Would that spur growth? That's the crux of hydroponics... to grow plants in a non-soil medium that provides better nutrition for faster growth... much faster... 3-5 times faster compared to soil. Coupled with increased duration of appropriate artificial light, the growth rate would go up further. Now when we are talking about the hydroponic technique where plants can grow many times faster, why isn't this the norm? Why don't we grow everything through this route? Can all greens be grown this way? What are the giveaways and takeaways?

This book will expose the reader to all that is required to know, including several hidden, untold truths of hydroponics, to enable practicing hydroponics very profitably, easily at a commercial scale, or as a hobby.

———◆◆———

Hydroponics is not new. Some say the Hanging Gardens of Babylon may have used this same technique. The omnipresent and very basic Lucky Bamboo plants are the simplest form of hydroponic plants. Lucky Bamboo plants have their stems immersed in water, and roots grow into water to suck nutrients from the water. Pothos, which is more commonly known as money plants, are domestic favorites to be kept in water bottles, with all their nutrition coming just from water. Ever been to the backwaters of Kerala? You'll see plenty of plants floating on water. These plants do not need any soil or fertilizer. They just float and grow on water and suck nutrients from the water. The point here is that hydroponics is natural and naturally abundant in the environment that surrounds us. It's not something that is coming from the lab. It's nature's gift. What we'll be doing is learning how to apply this natural science to grow bountiful veggies that are normally grown in soil.

Whatever one does should be driven by reason.

Reason is not universal.

Individuals are unique and carry their own perspective on things that matter to them.

An individual's perspective can be shaped by need.

What can be the need for hydroponics?

Need to do a very lucrative commercial project, with payback in as little as just a year, with just a little learning.

Or the need for one to develop a hobby that's not mundane, but a bit challenging, a bit rewarding, a bit experimental.

Or the need for one to grow within the constraints of space, as in urban living.

Or the need to surround oneself with the vibrance of profusely growing greens, where growth is multiple times faster, can be seen on a nearly daily basis.

Or the need to grow one's own veggies, having the satisfaction of knowing that they are pesticide-free.

Or the need for someone to grow veggies predictably and reliably, negating the whims of weather.

Or need to *surely* grow veggies, frustrated with vagaries experienced in conventional gardening.

Or the need for one to immerse in something that's the future of farming, potentially becoming a professional occupation.

Or simply the need to try out something new.

Hydroponics is *all of the above*.

And extremely profitable when practiced at a commercial scale.

All or any of the above can be your reason to pick this book.

It's rewarding.

Hydroponics is:

- Easy to learn and easy to apply for hobby or profitable commercial ventures

- For much faster plant growth – can be seen on a daily basis. Growth is what manifests as an exhilarating experience, apart from being more profitable

- Space-friendly. Does not require vast farmlands. Just a fraction is needed

- Can be started small or big. Easily scalable, as more space becomes available

- Quality of the produce is high and fetches a premium. The leaves and fruits are bigger

- Low labor

- Practically pesticide-free

- Possible in small places - apartment owners, city life, rooftops, basements

- Done outdoors as well as in indoor controlled environments – prevents loss from hailstorms, rain, and weather changes

- Fertilizer friendly – as in hydroponics, fertilizer consumption efficiency is high compared to use in soil. Ensures more mindful consumption of fertilizers

- No smell due to manure or organic decaying matter

- Profoundly profitable and all green when coupled with solar power

- Predictable profits & consistent results

- Future-proof. Hydroponics will grow as the climate turns harsher, as it will

A few hydroponic images are appended toward the end of the book to give you a feel. Or simply turn the page and start off.

To start, first let us know this wee bit about hydroponics:

Hydroponics is a technique to grow plants *without soil.*

Roots pull nutrition from an aqueous medium (called hydroponic solution) – that is, water + nutrients.

Air is very important for roots, so air is bubbled into this hydroponic solution.

Heat adversely impacts plant growth. It is necessary to keep the hydroponic solution cool, below 25°C to a maximum of 30°C.

Light is important for plants to grow. Sunlight is the best. Artificial grow lights are used to grow indoors.

pH of the hydroponic solution is important. Has to be <6.5.

Concentration of nutrients is important.

Water hardness is important.

Quality and composition of nutrients are important.

Humidity is important.

All this is easily manageable. It's not rocket science.

Several of the above aspects can be automatically taken care of.

Everything will be explained in subsequent sections.

Hydroponics can be an extremely profitable business venture, without many complications such as the availability of farmland, uncertainty due to weather, and the excruciating labor of farmlands. It's easy.

Just about everyone loves gardening, we know. The joy of seeing the plants grow is unparalleled.

It'll be explained how this joy can be magnified easily by practicing hydroponics – commercially or at home.

Hydroponics Explained

There are numerous types of hydroponic techniques and systems. It would be overwhelming and possibly disinteresting to suddenly dive into all those types with an exhaustive explanation of those systems. That is probably one reason why hydroponics is currently not as popular as it deserves to be. Details of the myriad hydroponic systems are available in exceedingly vast detail online and tend to inundate the reader, leaving them flummoxed regarding what could be the appropriate hydroponic path to follow.

Here, the approach would be to first understand the principle and working of one common system; then all others can be easily understood sequentially in later parts of the book. It's important to get started on a sprint and then gain momentum gradually as we proceed with a better understanding of the concepts involved.

The image below shows a highly effective and popular hydroponic system called Deep Water Culture (DWC).

This will be used to understand the concepts easily.

All parts of the hydroponic system will be discussed in detail subsequently, but the first task is to familiarize with the basics, for which this image is sufficient. Read the text carefully to understand the function of the various components. The same concepts apply at any scale – hobby or commercial.

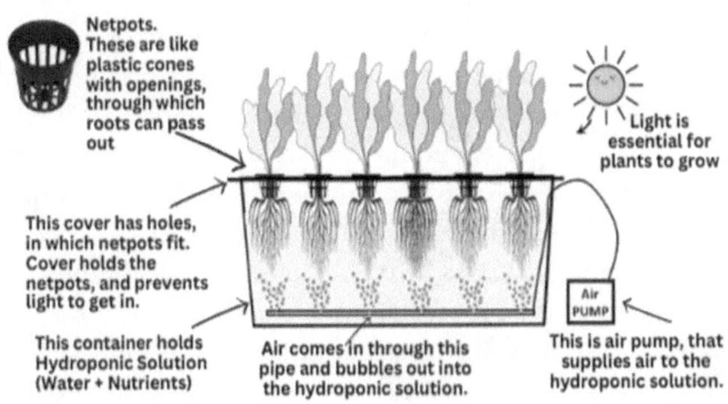

This system is called DEEP WATER CULTURE (DWC) because it contains a relatively deep level of hydroponic solution (i.e., water + nutrients) in the system, such that the roots of plants are dangling inside the hydroponic solution.

The idea is that the plants are placed in the small, netted containers called net pots, and the plant roots pass out through the holes in the net pots to dangle in the solution below. The solution is contained inside a container - or in other systems in channels or pipes. The solution has nutrients dissolved in it that provide the entire nutrition needed by plants, and the light does the rest for rapid growth of plants. Why hydroponics leads to multiple times better growth compared to soil can be self-evident. In hydroponics, the entire surface area of roots is exposed to useful nutrients and water, whereas in soil, the roots need to expend energy - to pick their way through the soil to 'find' nutrients suitable for their growth. In hydroponics, roots catch all the nutrients they need for the plant to grow without having to find them – no hindrance – no dearth, so the plants grow like mad. A common question is why the hydroponic solution does not rot. That's because air is being pumped in. Air keeps the solution fresh – for months altogether.

First, the plant saplings are grown separately from seeds, in just cocopeat and made ready for transplanting them in a hydroponic system. Cocopeat is readily & cheaply available – it is in the form of beaten down small pieces of coconut husk fiber and is an excellent growing medium. Cocopeat is inert, being pH neutral. That means it's neither acidic nor basic. Seeds grow best in a neutral pH environment. To grow the saplings from seeds, cocopeat is available as compressed tiny disks that expand to 5 times their volume when soaked in water. These cocopeat disks are commonly called Jiffy Plugs and have a thin fine mesh fabric that keeps the cocopeat together – making them the most convenient and mess-free means of growing seeds into saplings. Saplings sprout on their own from seeds, without any need for nutrients – as long as the cocopeat is kept moist and warm. Sometime later on, you may refer to the recommended growing conditions for various types of seeds given in the later part of the book. A common mistake people make while growing seeds is to push them too deep into cocopeat. Don't push them too deep; otherwise, they will not sprout. A good rule of thumb is to keep the depth of seeds equal to the size of seeds. The bigger the seeds, the deeper they should be planted inside cocopeat. The smaller the seed, the shallower their depth should be.

Jiffy plugs look like this.

On the left are 4 pieces of dry Jiffy Plugs, as they were bought.

On the right is a Jiffy Plug expanded 5 times after being soaked in water.

Rockwool cubes are also commonly sold in the hydroponic market to grow seeds into seedlings. Rockwool is not pH neutral and needs to be added with some pH control additive. Rockwool isn't safe on hands and requires wearing gloves while using them. There are a few foreign companies that have developed rockwool into safe & convenient growing cubes through their proprietary know-how, but those are quite expensive. Any cheaper versions are bound to be a look-alike and not genuine. Why go with rockwool cubes when Jiffy Plugs are available cheaply, easily, and do the job well.

When the saplings have sprouted, wait for the first 2-3 true leaves to develop before adding some very dilute, low-strength nutrients. Thereafter, wait for the saplings to develop a few more leaves and grow into reasonably strong saplings, about 3-4 inches tall, before transplanting them into the hydroponic system.

To transplant saplings into the hydroponic system, the coco peat needs to be washed away gently from the roots. This needs to be done with gentle hands to prevent root breakage. Remove the outer fabric of the Jiffy Plugs that hold the saplings. Then gently pour water on the coco peat to see it simply getting washed away. Saplings with exposed roots are then planted into the net pots.

Net pots look like this.

Net pots are like tiny plastic baskets with openings through which the roots can come out and dangle into the hydroponic solution below. Net pots have a wider-rim that keeps them in place in the hydroponic system and prevents them from falling down into the system. The rim of the net pots bears all the weight of the plant, so wider-rim net pots are better. Net pots are generally 2-inch or 3-inch in size. A 2-inch size suffices for most plants, unless the objective is to grow really big plants like the indeterminate variety of tomato – that keeps growing endlessly. Gently place the sapling with its roots toward the bottom of the net pots while the stem comes out through the top. Leaves remain out of the net pots. Saplings need to be supported inside the net pots, for which purpose LECA balls are used. LECA is Light Expanded Clay Aggregate and is commonly available. It is lightweight, porous, and has some water absorption capacity. LECA should be first soaked in the hydroponic solution and then the soaked LECA should be dropped inside the net pots around the stem of the saplings – to support the stem from all sides and to provide them nourishment in the initial phase of development.

In any kind of a hydroponic system, care should be exercised to ensure that only the plant roots are submerged in the hydroponic solution. The plant stem should mainly remain above the solution, and this can be achieved by ensuring the saplings are not pushed too deep down in net pots. The hydroponic solution is hypertonic and may cause stem rot in some plants. This issue is not noticeable in 2-inch net pots but can occur in larger net pots of 3 inches or above. When placing the saplings in net pots, do not push the entire stem to the base of the net pot. Position them so that the roots start from nearly the middle of the net pot. If part of the roots remains above the waterline, that's okay as long as some portions of the roots are submerged to prevent the risk of roots drying out.

After the saplings are planted into the net pots, do not straightaway expose them to direct sun. Keep them in partial shade for 2-3 days, preferably, so that the saplings get accustomed to their new environment and do not experience shock. This approach is better for their survival. Despite everything, a few saplings may not survive the transplanting process. For this reason, it's advisable to prepare a few extra saplings in net pots compared to the slots available in your hydroponic system.

The hydroponic system by itself is a container that holds the hydroponic solution, covered by a cover that has holes in it. Holes are cut into the cover using a drill machine called a holesaw.

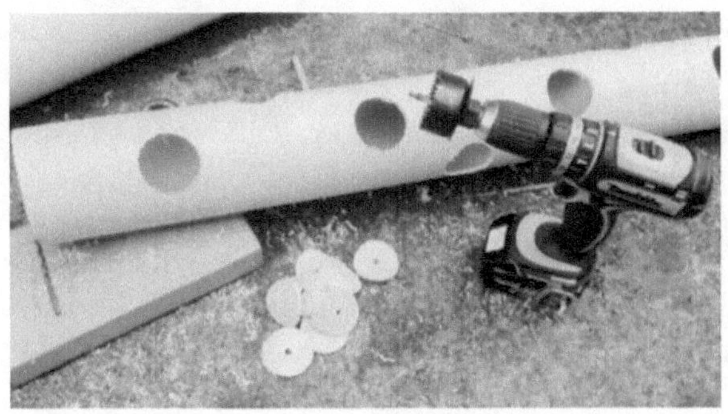

A holesaw is a drilling machine where circular bits are attached that come in different sizes. When using 2-inch net pots, use a 51 mm diameter holesaw bit. Similarly, for other net pot sizes, choose the size of holesaw bit accordingly. Be very careful while operating the holesaw. It's safe if used with care in experienced hands. For a novice, it's better to seek a carpenter's services. The same holesaw is used whether cutting into a wooden board, wooden ply, plastic PVC pipes, or PVC channels. When using the holesaw for a long duration, it gets hot due to the friction of cutting through surfaces, causing it to expand – which can make the successive holes slightly bigger with the same holesaw drill bit. It is advisable to take some rest when cutting holes and let the drill bit cool in between after repeated cuts. Alternatively, dip it in water intermittently to cool it down before resuming further cutting. A good rule is to make the holes for 2-inch net pots about 6-7 inches apart, center to center.

It is necessary to attach an air pump that pushes air into the hydroponic solution resident inside the tank. Increasing the quantity of air is directly beneficial and better for plant growth. The more air pumped in, the more plant growth there will be. The more bubbling movement in the hydroponic solution, the better it becomes for washing the roots – for better growth. Consider placing the air pump in a manner that circulates the hydroponic solution as much as possible – that's good for plant growth.

Light is essential for saplings to grow. Sunlight is best, as long as the ambient air temperature is below 35 degrees Celsius. Otherwise, indoor grow lights are used in a controlled environment.

As the saplings grow, their roots consume water plus nutrients from the hydroponic solution, requiring occasional replenishment of nutrients and water in the hydroponic solution tank. As the roots are fully exposed to water, nutrition, and air, they develop much faster compared to soil plants, leading to extraordinary growth of plants.

Hydroponic solution is made by adding nutrients to the water. Nutrients are pre-mixed solids that are available in several forms by several companies and contain 100% of the nutrition required by plants. All the nutrition necessary for plant growth is present in the hydroponic nutrients. Nutrients contain Calcium, Magnesium, Nitrogen, Phosphorus, Potassium, Iron, Copper, Molybdenum, Boron, Manganese, Zinc, Sodium, and Sulfur. Putting all these nutrients in a single mixture causes them to react with each other, causing nutrient lock, rendering them useless. That is the reason for all commercially available nutrients to come as 2-Part solutions or 3-Part solutions, which means the nutrients that can react with each other in concentrated form are separated into 2 or 3 separate bottles. They do not react with each other in diluted form – as in the hydroponic solution that's made after adding nutrients to water.

Water used in hydroponics needs to be soft water. Water hardness is measured as TDS, which stands for Total Dissolved Solids. Water has its own TDS depending on where the water is sourced. Hard water is detrimental to plants, so the lower the water TDS, the better. Only the TDS resulting from hydroponic nutrients is beneficial for plants.

pH of the hydroponic solution is also a very important parameter. The pH needs to be kept between 4 and 6.5. The pH generally tends to increase over time, and growers need to add pH Down solution to bring down the pH whenever it crosses 6.5.

Humidity is also important. Generally, high humidity is not an issue for most plants, but low-humidity would tend to desiccate the plants.

All these topics will be covered in detail subsequently. First, we'll explain the various types of hydroponic systems next.

——◆◆——

Types of Hydroponic Systems

Now armed with a reasonable familiarization of the operation of a functional hydroponic system, let's introduce the various types of hydroponic system configurations that have evolved due to varying priorities among users.

If the electrical power supply is not reliable in one's neighborhood, the hydroponic user may have the priority that the plants should not be impacted, even if power is not there for a couple of hours.

If the water supply in one's neighborhood has high TDS, meaning hard water, then the hydroponic user would tend to use a system that minimizes water consumption so that its functioning remains unaffected by high salts in solution.

The hydroponic may generally have life priorities elsewhere, thereby preferring a hydroponic system that requires minimal supervision and can continue even if it's left unattended for a few days. This is an important consideration, as hydroponics need not be an all-involving occupation.

A hydroponic grower using expensive nutrients would tend to use a system that minimizes nutrient wastage while ensuring complete consumption of those nutrients.

If real estate is the paramount constraint, that would become the major driver for the selection of the type of system that consumes less space.

Someone living in a hot climate zone would have priority to adopt a hydroponic system that remains relatively unaffected by the heatwaves.

The type of plants to be grown impacts the choice of systems selected. Some plants have big roots, requiring hydroponic systems that can accommodate big roots, which can otherwise choke systems with a tiny root zone.

Installation cost is a survival factor for commercial hydroponic growers.

Ease of use is generally the primary influencing factor for hobby hydroponic enthusiasts.

These are just a few variations that can change the choice of the system.

Necessity is the mother of invention, as the adage goes, and holds quite pertinent in the current context of hydroponics.

Necessity imposed due to constraints or preferences becomes the driver for the development of choices and alternatives.

That's how it generally is in life, and so it is in hydroponics. As the requirements change and as the technology advances, developments emerge in the form of newer designs. New people coming into this field bring fresh perspectives, which create further improvements in design, as surely you would too.

Hydroponic techniques and systems can be categorized into 8 types, listed generally in the order of increasing complexity. Several variations have been created over time by extending or combining these hydroponic types.

1. Wick systems

2. Media Bed

3. Flood & Drain (Ebb & Flow)

4. Deep Water Culture (DWC)

5. Drip systems

6.   Nutri Film Technique (NFT)

7.   Aeroponics

8.   Aquaponics

Most basic ones are described first, followed by ones in increasing order of complexity and performance. The higher the complexity, generally the better the performance, but increased complexity introduces issues of its own. That's the trade-off – simplicity versus performance. But it does not mean that simpler systems are not recommended. With increasing complexity, the maintenance and cost increase, as does the risk of non-functionality due to some part of the complex system becoming dysfunctional. So, every system has its own benefits and drawbacks. Most commercial hydroponic systems generally adopt the middle ones – either Deep Water Culture (DWC) or Nutri Film Technique (NFT).

Nutrient management will be discussed separately and exclusively in a later chapter, as it is common to all the hydroponic systems.

Wick Systems

A wick is something that everyone has seen at some point.

A wick is the cord, the thread, which runs through the center of the candle and burns at the candle tip.

A wick is any bundle of cotton fibers, which is twisted and loosely braided or woven together and has absorbent characteristics. The wick absorbs the liquid and transfers it to its top by capillary action. In a candle, the wick thread that runs through the center of the candle absorbs the liquid wax and transfers it to its burning tip – that keeps the candle burning.

Similarly, wicking material is used in the wick-type hydroponic systems to transfer the hydroponic solution residing in the container to the plants above. Unlike the wick of a candle, the wick used in the hydroponic systems is thicker - made of materials as simple as rope, string, or felt. The thicker the wick, the easier it becomes for capillary action to happen.

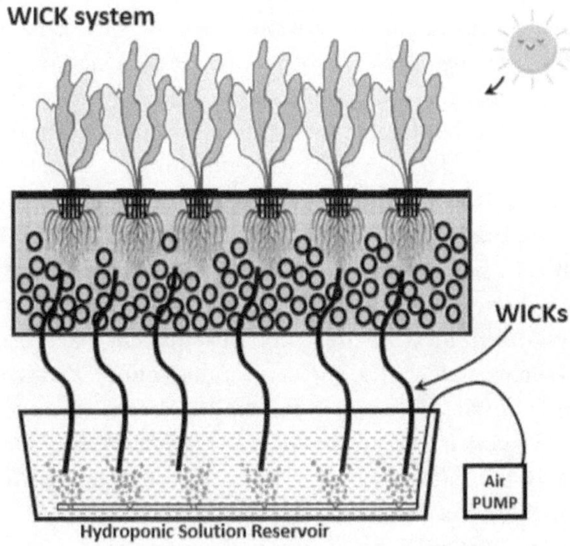

Wick hydroponic systems are a very simple and easy version of hydroponics. Functionally, it's actually a self-watering pot, now so commonly used in home gardening.

Wick hydroponic systems are divided into 2 portions – Upper and Lower. These 2 portions are connected by the wicks. The upper portion is the growing tray that holds growing media with plants, while the lower portion acts as the reservoir to hold the hydroponic solution. Wicks are immersed in the hydroponic solution, acting like conduits for transferring the hydroponic solution from the lower portion to the upper portion. Water and nutrients that form the hydroponic solution slowly move up the wick and saturate the growing media around the root systems of the plants above. The bigger the system, the more wicks are required to cover the entire volume of the growing media. For every plant in the growing medium bed, it is advisable to have a wick close by running from the lower reservoir. Placing multiple wicks and placing them particularly close to the plant root systems helps.

Being immersed in the hydroponic solution, wicks act like a sponge to absorb water and nutrients from the solution and transfer them to the upper portion where the wick is in contact with the growing media. A noteworthy aspect here is that for the Wick system hydroponics to work, the growing media bed above needs to be suitable – meaning it should have the ability to pick and transfer the water-nutrients from the wick to spread them onwards across the growing bed. Coco Peat, Perlite, and vermiculite are excellent growing mediums for the purpose. Any kind of absorbing fibrous material can also serve well as growing media. Fibers or husk drawn from the outer shell of coconuts are considered ideal as they are pH neutral, have excellent moisture retention ability, and can conduct nutrient transference efficiently. Perlite is also good for similar reasons and is also pH neutral, making it suitable for wicking systems. Perlite is reusable repeatedly but carries a higher upfront cost compared to coco peat medium. Vermiculite is also suitable and it possesses a high capacity to store nutrients for use over time.

If you are already initiated into hydroponics, you may wonder why LECA (Lightweight Expanded Clay Aggregate) balls have not been mentioned here. LECA balls have excellent porosity, absorption, and offer very good voidage. LECA is cleanable, reusable, lightweight, and drains well while retaining moisture too. LECA is the top choice for all kinds of hydroponics due to these reasons. But <u>not</u> in wick hydroponic systems. A bed of LECA balls when in contact with the wick does not successfully participate in the wicking action. That's because only a very tiny surface of LECA balls can touch the wick, and that limits its ability to suck away water from the wick, making it unsuitable for wick hydroponic systems.

A practical problem in wick systems is that over time, salts deposit on the wick and gradually reduce its capacity to facilitate the transfer of water and nutrients to the upper zone. Wicking action is also slow and sometimes unable to cope with the water and nutrient requirements of the plants – this can happen if the plants are large in size. Oxygen availability for the roots is limited by whatever voidage remains in the bed after it is saturated with the water that is drawn up through the wick – hence limited. Compaction of the bed over time or due to binding of the bed by roots further reduces the oxygen availability to the roots. That is why plant growth in wick systems is not as spectacular as can be expected in other advanced types of hydroponic systems. To enhance aeration, an air pump may be added to the wick system's reservoir, which keeps aerating the hydroponic solution and somewhat aids in augmenting the oxygen supply to the plant roots.

Wick hydroponic systems fall into the category of passive hydroponics, which means that there are no moving parts like mechanical pumps to transfer or circulate the hydroponic solution. Since these systems do not have any moving parts, they do not need an electrical supply, except for an air pump (if used).

This is a reasonable option for beginners to start exploring hydroponics.

Benefits of Wick Systems

Ease of use: A wick system is a very simple set-up and can easily be put together by anyone. It doesn't require any attention after it has been set-up. It just requires that the hydroponic solution in the bottom reservoir be regularly topped up, and it will keep running on its own, practically as a hands-off operating system. The wicks will continuously keep supplying the hydroponic solution to the plants, and the plants will keep growing with no risk of them drying out – unless, of course, the wicks become insufficient to cope with the water loss happening via transpiration through the leaves of big plants. Suited only for smallish plants like Lettuce, Spinach, Basil, Herbs.

No Electricity: These systems do not require any electricity to run, which saves costs.

Consumes little space: All the space that these systems need is the space needed to place them. As the hydroponic solution container is located just below the growing bed, it's like a double story and hence space efficient. No space is consumed for the electrical pump installation. It can be placed practically anywhere without the need to locate them close to an electrical power source. They do not require drainage very often, which again reduces the hassle of locating the drainpipe.

No pesticides: This is the repeating theme for all kinds of hydroponic systems. In all kinds of hydroponics, soil-borne pests are absent, though pesticides may still be needed for airborne pests like mealy bugs, aphids, and thrips - which can be handled well by organic neem spray. Commercial growers sometimes release ladybirds in their polyhouse, and each ladybird can eat 200-400 eggs every day – obviating the need for even neem spray. No pesticide applies to all hydroponic types, hence we will not repeat it hereafter.

Drawbacks of Wick Systems

Plant growth is not phenomenal: Hydroponics is performed to experience the joy of fast-growing plants, but that's lacking in these wick systems. Plant growth would be faster than in soil, but only marginally.

Suits small plants only: Small plants like basil, lettuce, spinach, and herbs such as mint and rosemary grow well in these systems. However, big plants like tomatoes, brinjal, and vines like gourds do not fare well in these systems due to reasons mentioned earlier, such as their high demand for water and nutrients. As the growing bed remains perpetually moist, that also becomes a limitation for some plants. Root vegetables like turnips and carrots do not thrive in these systems.

Limited Oxygen to Roots: These systems do not offer much opportunity to enhance the oxygen availability to roots, leaving the user constrained. Plant growth is hence not spectacular.

Susceptible to Rot: The growing bed in this system always remains moist and humid – which is not a problem in other hydroponic systems, but it becomes a problem in this system due to the limited availability of oxygen, leading to the risk of fungal outbreaks and rot.

Nutrient Accumulation: Over time, the nutrients coming along with water as drawn up by the wick settle in the growing bed and wicks; they keep accumulating. There's no way of knowing how many nutrients have accumulated and how many have been consumed. Wicking action gets poorer as time passes, making the performance of the system quite unpredictable.

Overall, the wick hydroponic systems are not the preferred way to do hydroponics, to put it bluntly.

⸺ ✦✦ ⸺

Media Bed

The Media Bed can easily be visualized as the top container/ growing bed of the previously described wick system – minus the wicks and reservoir. The Media Bed is a simple growing bed that contains inert media impregnated with hydroponic nutrient solution. It's the most basic of all types of hydroponics. It's actually just like a normal soil pot, except that inert media is used instead of soil. The inert media generally used are CocoPeat, coco coir fiber or vermiculite.

It's hydroponics in its simplest form, yet effective.

Media Bed

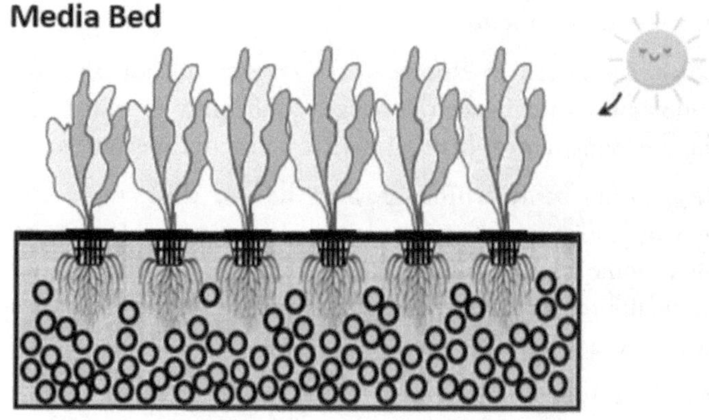

Media Bed does not have an automatic supply of hydroponic nutrients as happens in the wick systems. That's why the user needs to periodically supply the hydroponic solution to the media bed. As in wick systems, over time, the nutrients accumulate in the media bed and keep accumulating. That's because the plants do not consume as many nutrients as they consume water. As the hydroponic solution is supplied to the media bed through the top layer, over time, the accumulation of nutrients can become visible in the form of whitish deposits. This accumulation over time is not good for some plants like lettuce as they need constancy of nutrient composition in the root zone. However, some plants like tomatoes and spinach remain unaffected by this changing composition in the root zone.

An easy way to address this issue of nutrient accumulation is to occasionally *wash* the media bed by pouring lots of water on it and allowing the water to dissolve and drain out the accumulated nutrients – hence refreshing the bed entirely. The media bed has drain holes in the bottom, through which any excess solution/water flows out. Drain holes are essential as they also allow air to be drawn into the media bed. The ability to easily refresh the media bed after every few weeks makes it attractive. However, refreshing the bed every few weeks leads to nutrient loss.

To address the problem of nutrient loss and improve the consistency of nutrient composition in the media bed, there is a very effective method practiced by many commercial growers. Every 2-3 days, the media bed is sprayed or poured with hydroponic solution until it starts leaching out from the bottom drain holes. The leachate is collected and tested for TDS and pH to get an idea of the nutrient bed situation in the bottom layer of the bed. The top layer of the media bed is saturated with fresh nutrient, and the bottom layer has a slightly more concentrated nutrient situation. As the process is repeated every 2-3 days, there is largely a constancy of nutrient concentration in the media bed. Since the testing of leachate is done every 2-3 days, there is a fair knowledge of the nutrient concentration and its pH in the bed. This constancy is good for the health of the plants and their continued wellbeing. This method also allows the user to take proper preventive action. For example, if the user finds that the TDS of the leachate is considerably higher than the TDS of the fresh hydroponic solution, then the user may choose to reduce the strength of the fresh hydroponic solution that is being poured every 2-3 days on the bed. Alternatively, if the user finds that the TDS of the leachate is lower than the TDS of the fresh hydroponic solution, then the user would need to introduce a greater quantity of fresh hydroponic solution so that the bed gets saturated throughout with a higher TDS hydroponic solution. In a similar way, the user can monitor the pH of the media bed as well.

An important aspect of growing in a Media Bed is to practice *hiatus*... to observe periods of doing nothing. Sounds good!

What this means is that after saturating the media bed with hydroponic solution, leave it and do nothing. Allow the excess hydroponic solution to drain out. Let the media bed become partially dry. As the bed dries partially, it increases the available void spaces and draws in more air – which is very good for root development and root health. This holds especially true for the media beds using coco peat or coco coir – as they have a high water-holding capacity.

Media Bed hydroponics using coco peat is common. It can also be done using LECA balls and/or perlite in place of coco peat. That can yield somewhat better results but requires more care and automation. LECA balls and perlite do not have as much water-holding capacity as coco peat does. For perspective, coco peat will hold nearly 100% of water when compared to its own weight, while LECA balls will hold much less, approximately 15% water when compared with their own weight. Perlite will hold even less – typically 10% water when compared with its own weight. LECA balls and perlite offer very good mechanical strength for the roots to latch on to for binding and to grow on, but they do not offer high water retention capacity. LECA balls and perlite also offer very high voidage in the bed, which ensures very high air availability for the roots – that's excellent for roots. But LECA balls and perlite have low water retention and will dry up much earlier than coco peat. That's why media beds using LECA balls and/or perlite need to be doused with hydroponic solution more often compared to coco peat beds. The common practice is that the media beds using LECA balls and/or perlite need to be supplemented with an automated sprayer that sprays the hydroponic solution on the media bed every 30 minutes or so using timers, and leachate is re-circulated. The spray should cover the full surface of the bed. Such repeated spraying ensures the continued availability of nutrients and water to the roots in media beds using LECA balls and/or perlite. This cyclic spraying of hydroponic solution to the roots in media beds using LECA balls and/or perlite closely mimics the most advanced form of hydroponics called aeroponics – which will be explained toward the end of this section.

Performance of the media beds using LECA balls and/or perlite can be quite good, but despite being as easy as it sounds, it requires experience, and the system is a bit difficult to build. Leachate from the media bed needs to be collected, and then it needs to be pumped back to the media bed via conduits/ pipes - all the while ensuring that the light does not contact the hydroponic solution - to prevent the growth of algae. The spray assembly needs to be fixed on the bed so that it does not fall off or get misaligned and can continue to provide good coverage of the bed. Over time, nutrients would tend to deposit and choke the spray heads, requiring cleaning. If the electrical supply fails for a couple of hours, the plant roots will go dry and shrivel. A timer would be needed to routinely switch the pump on and off. Spraying generally causes some misting and hence evaporation. The user will have to top-up the hydroponic solution in the leachate collection reservoir occasionally. If it so happens that the pump runs without the hydroponic solution, the pump may burn out. The timer switching the pump on/off may generate some intermittent noise – which the user may find obtrusive to their living environment. If any low noise is continuous, we tend to get immune to it gradually and it becomes unnoticeable. But if any noise is intermittent even if it is low – like coming on and off rhythmically, it becomes difficult to ignore and possibly disconcerting. I've known people who got so irritated with the rhythmic on/offs of the pump that they pulled the timer out and threw it away.

Despite being the simplest form of hydroponics, media bed hydroponics can be very effective depending on the user's experience, protocol, and practice. Media Bed Hydroponics is practiced differently by different growers, as it offers complete flexibility to manipulate 'and control.

If someone does an online search for types of hydroponics, there's a good chance that media bed hydroponics will not come up in the results. Perhaps the reason for this is that online articles and publications are generally promoted by the manufacturers & sellers of the hydroponic equipment. What good would it do for any business to promote literature on media bed hydroponics, where minimal equipment is involved? Media Bed hydroponics is perhaps the most underrated and under-informed form of hydroponics, despite giving reasonably good results, simply because it does not come with equipment intricacies that can be commercialized or monetized.

Media Bed Hydroponics is suitable for all plant types and becomes the only choice for root plants like beetroot, radish, carrot, and potato. That's a key differentiator of Media Bed, as the root plants are not possible to grow in most other types of hydroponic systems. But in Media Bed, root development mimics the root development as would happen in a normal kind of soil bed.

A problem that can occur in a Media Bed is the risk of salt accumulation on plant roots. To prevent this from happening, washing the bed entirely once every few days until lots of leachate comes out, and then restarting with a fresh solution to drench the bed, is the satisfactory method employed.

Media Bed is hassle-free. When it uses coco peat, growth is not stupendous. But if LECA balls are used with automatic sprays (described previously), then it becomes like the most advanced aeroponic hydroponic system.

There is an associated interesting topic of 'Semi-hydroponics' that deserves to be elaborated when discussing media bed hydroponics.

Semi-hydroponics is also referred to as 'semi-hydro', or sometimes called hydroculture and is getting quite a bit of attention recently. It's popular among hobby growers for growing ornamental plants like peace lilies and pothos inside their homes. It's quite useful and popular for growing orchid plants, provided the right humid environment can be maintained.

Semi-hydroponics is a slight variation of media beds using LECA balls. A bowl or small container – without any holes, is filled with LECA balls and then hydroponic solution is poured on the LECA balls. Plant saplings are placed inside LECA Ball beds inside these balls, and the plant roots gradually grow to encompass the LECA balls over time. A bit of hydroponic solution is left accumulated at the bottom of the bowl; it serves to keep the LECA balls moist through capillary action. Capillary action can transfer the hydroponic solution just 4-5 inches above, so the functionality of Semi-hydroponics is limited to small bowls and for indoor kind of ornamental plants that do not consume much water. A weak hydroponic solution is normally used in such a Semi-hydroponic bowl as they do not have any drainage, and there is no easy provision to wash the LECA balls. Air availability to the roots is as good as in normal media beds using LECA balls. These kinds of Semi-hydroponic systems are not meant for growing vegetables as they cannot support the water & nutrient demand of fast-growing veggies. These systems are used for growing small ornamental plants only - in glass containers filled with LECA balls with a little hydroponic solution sitting at its base. A glass vase with LECA balls surrounded by roots amplifies the beauty of the plant, and that's its purpose.

Deep Water Culture

Deep Water Culture (DWC) is a type of hydroponic cultivation where the plant roots are suspended or floating in the hydroponic solution. This system has already been briefly touched upon in the earlier chapter when introducing the subject of hydroponics, and here are the details.

This is one of the easiest and most popular methods of hydroponics, very prevalent among hobby hydroponic enthusiasts as well as commercial growers. This is a very good choice for commercial hydroponics; economic rationale is presented through case studies in the 'Commercial' section later.

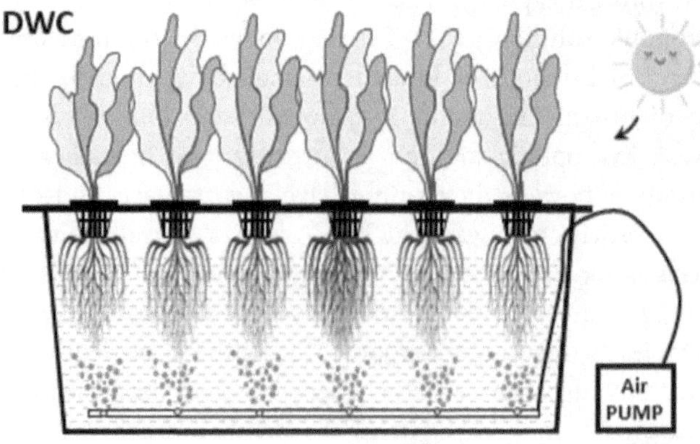

This system comprises a reservoir that holds the hydroponic solution, with a top board that covers the reservoir. Holes are punched in the cover, and net pots are placed inside these holes. Plant saplings are planted in the net pots, supported by LECA balls, where the plants grow and their roots pass through the mesh of the net pots to dangle down into the hydroponic solution.

Generally, the depth of the reservoir is selected to suit the plants that are to be grown. The bigger the roots of the plants, the higher the selected depth. Typically, a depth of anything more than 8-10 inches serves well for all kinds of plants. The more the depth of the reservoir, the more the volume of the hydroponic solution that can be stored inside it. The greater the hydroponic solution storage, the more convenient it becomes for the grower to manage the nutrient solution – this aspect will be explained in detail later under the nutrient management section.

As the plant roots are submerged inside the hydroponic solution, the roots get continuous access to the nutrition they need, along with getting the water and oxygen they need to grow.

It is imperative to oxygenate the hydroponic solution resident inside the reservoir. Without oxygenation, roots will rot. Oxygenation is done using air pumps that push air from the surrounding ambiance into the hydroponic solution in the form of bubbles, thereby creating an oxygen-rich nutrient solution. Different types of air pumps are available; generally, the common aquarium pumps are well suited for the purpose. Some air pumps are submerged type, which means the pump itself is sitting inside the water and it draws air from outside – air getting drawn in by the force of water being thrown ahead by the pump. Submerged type pumps are extremely effective as they also circulate the hydroponic solution. Circulation of the hydroponic solution helps in improved growth of the plants. Systems where the solution is circulated around inside are called circulating type hydroponic systems and give better results compared to systems where the solution is not circulated but only gets oxygenated through passing air bubbles into it. Another type of air pump is the external type, where the air pump stays outside the hydroponic system, and it pumps air inside the solution via a pipe. An air stone connected to the end of the air pipe makes fine air bubbles that oxygenate the solution. Air pumps cannot pump air too far below the liquid level unless they are designed for it. Select an air pump that can work well with the depth of the reservoir being used. Typically, all air pumps can pump air till a 6-8 inch depth – which is sufficient for the purpose. Bubbling the air also helps in agitating the solution, which helps in preventing any risk of salt accumulation on plant roots.

There's a relatively lesser-known fact about air bubbling, which is that air bubbling can impact the temperature of the hydroponic solution. Suppose the hydroponic system is kept in a hot ambiance with hot air around. Bubbling that hot air inside the hydroponic solution will increase the temperature of the hydroponic solution. High temperature is the worst enemy of hydroponics. When the temperature of the hydroponic solution crosses 30 degrees Celsius, it becomes nearly impossible for the plant roots to pick up nutrients from water – and the plant growth stunts. As the temperature of the hydroponic solution increases, the solubility of oxygen also decreases. The solubility of oxygen in water nearly halves at 30 degrees Celsius compared to its solubility at 10 degrees Celsius. In other words, water can hold less oxygen at higher temperatures, and more oxygen at lower temperatures. Due to this reason, even if someone pumps in lots of air inside a hot hydroponic solution, the hydroponic solution will not absorb much oxygen. A high temperature of the solution is not good for plants in the hydroponic solution.

If the hot ambient air is at 40 degrees Celsius and it's bubbled inside the hydroponic solution, it will increase the temperature of the solution. This is an aspect that's relatively unnoticed among the growers. Now let's look at it another way. Suppose you are a hobby grower and have your DWC hydroponic system kept on your balcony surrounded by hot summer air. If you just manage to relocate the air inlet of your air pump from inside a nearby air-conditioned room, that small amount of air-conditioned air drawn from inside your air-conditioned room will actually cool down the hydroponic solution kept on your adjacent balcony. Read this sentence again and appreciate its importance. Hydroponics allows one to think and innovate, something lacking in normal growing. Just by cooling the bubbling air, one can reduce the temperature of their hydroponic solution, obviating the need to fully air condition the entire apparatus or the room. This can be a very good option in commercial hydroponics.

A significant benefit in DWC systems is that even if the electrical power goes off for a couple of hours or even for a full day, there's no harm to the plants. It's common practice to switch off the air pump during nighttime and switch it back on during daytime. Switching it off for 12 hours or so is fine, and the hydroponic solution remains well charged with oxygen for that duration with the roots doing fine. This ability to switch off the power during nighttime without causing any impact to plants is beneficial in saving power costs, especially in big setups. During nighttime, plant metabolism and growth anyway go down, so no harm done. When pursuing indoor hydroponics using artificial lights, it does help to keep everything running for a longer duration as the plant growth keeps on - even during nighttime due to the presence of artificial lights. If the objective is to maximize plant growth within the shortest possible time, then running air all through the nighttime is fine.

In other hydroponic systems that will be discussed subsequently, there is a high dependency on the availability of electrical power, and the plants suffer if the power goes off even for a short duration. DWC hydroponic setups do not face this crunch and are hence a preferred choice of operation among a vast number of hydroponic growers – hobbyists and professionals.

DWC systems are quite easy to assemble and are relatively inexpensive. These systems do not need automation or expensive control equipment. Practically any container can be converted into a DWC system – even a bucket or any water tank. The good part of DWC hydroponics is that it can be scaled up easily with the application of absolutely the same concepts. A hobby grower can easily progress to professional DWC hydroponics by using the same experience and concepts, just applied at a bigger level. Professional growers have cost considerations as the paramount factor for their survival; that's where DWC systems score big.

Raft System

To further lower their costs, professional growers make wide channels to contain the hydroponic solution and cover it with rafts. The raft system is exactly a DWC system but with a cover that floats on the surface of the hydroponic solution. The raft is made of Styrofoam or a similar material that is reasonably strong and floats on the water surface. Holes are punched into the floating raft and net pots containing saplings are placed inside these holes. The rest of the functioning is exactly the same as for any DWC system. The raft has only so much buoyancy as the Styrofoam can provide. Too much weight on it will drown it. The raft is cheaper, but it can support only small plants like lettuce, spinach, some herbs – unlike a true DWC system with a cover that supports any plant of any size.

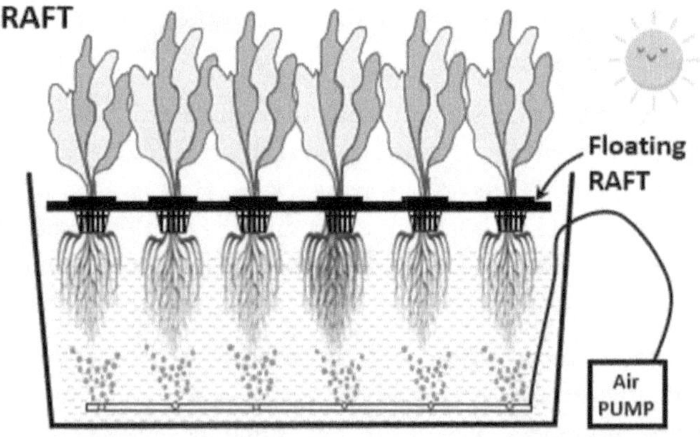

Another important fact about DWC systems, generally not known to people, is that these systems can be built with a high volume-to-surface ratio. What this means is that to grow the same number of plants, a DWC system can have much less of the system's surface area exposed to outside air – compared to other advanced systems that will be discussed subsequently. Surface area – how is that important – one may wonder! Already mentioned earlier is the fact that high temperature is the worst enemy of hydroponics. The temperature of the hydroponic system increases due to the hot ambiance, which is a direct function of the amount of surface area exposed to hot air. The more surface area the hydroponic system has, the more heat it will absorb from the surrounding hot air. Pipes and channels are extensively used in the NFT or aeroponic systems (covered next), while deep reservoirs are used in the DWC system. Deep reservoirs have much less surface area exposed to air compared to pipes and channels, allowing the DWC systems to remain relatively cooler compared to their NFT or aeroponic counterparts.

Talking of the high temperature menace, DWC offers one more opportunity to rein in the temperature increase in the hydroponic system. Using a wooden plank/board/ply material for the reservoir cover further reduces the heat ingress into the system. Wood is a good insulator and acts well to shield the reservoir from radiant heat due to the incident sunrays. Extending the same wooden cover beyond the reservoir edges by a few inches further helps in shading the reservoir below. Shade is better for the reservoir compared to incident sunrays from a temperature control perspective. Shielding the reservoir from all sides to provide shade to it further helps in preventing temperature rise.

By combining all the aforementioned aspects, it is possible to achieve good hydroponic performance in outdoor DWC hydroponic systems even in hot summers, without any climate control. It is very expensive to provide climate control for hydroponic systems, as that requires placing them inside a greenhouse with air-conditioning. DWC hydroponic systems perform well in this regard even outdoors, simply by focusing on minimizing heat ingress into the system.

DWC systems suit all plant types. This is another key differentiator. After having invested considerably in other types of hydroponic systems, users find that they can generally grow only small plant types in the small-bore channels and pipes used in other systems.

But in DWC systems, all plant types can be grown – smaller as well as big – in the same system. DWC systems are hence extremely versatile, and one can relax having the confidence of growing any plant in them. Tomatoes have huge root systems, which get accommodated very well in DWC systems. Similarly, vines like bottle gourd, bitter gourd and the like are huge plants that have big root systems and consume lots of water & nutrients – which is practically very difficult to supply in other hydroponic systems but do extremely well in DWC systems.

DWC systems are not promoted by the hydroponic equipment suppliers.

Obviously, why should they?

There isn't enough meat in DWC systems from a business viewpoint.

Hydroponic equipment suppliers make money from supplying the equipment, while there is not much equipment involved in DWC systems to sell. Money comes from selling the parts and pieces that can be joined together to form an exotic-looking structure – one that stands out from the crowd. That's what most people fall for and end up buying - the pipes and pieces that become difficult to clean or to operate after a few months. DWC systems just have a reservoir and its cover that can qualify as equipment. DWC systems do not use any pipes or channels. DWC systems can very well directly sit on the ground itself and do not need any structures to support them. When the equipment supplier does not have pipes or channels or a structure to sell in the name of a hydroponic system, where does the fellow make money from? That's the reason DWC systems are never advertised.

DWC systems also have another positive point in their favor. They do not have any leakage points. Other complicated systems like NFT or aeroponics (discussed next) are made by joining together a multitude of pipes and channels, with their water delivery mechanisms via plastic tubes fitting into the channels via jointers – necessitating a plethora of joints, any one of which can leak at any time. But DWC systems do not have any pipes or channels or jointers, so they do not have any leakage points. DWC systems remain leak-free practically for eternity. The only part that may need replacement after a few crop cycles is the top wooden cover – as it may sometimes bend due to the weight of the heavy plants – that is also resolved if a good-quality cover is chosen in the first place.

Another favorable point… net pots of any size can be used in the DWC systems – be it 2-inch net pots or 3-inch net pots. Some growers use a combination of different-sized net pots within the same DWC hydroponic system. 2-inch net pots are actually fine for all kinds of plants, but it's a matter of preference. Growers tend to use 3-inch net pots for the indeterminate variety of tomato plants whose stem keeps growing over time, so they do not have to worry about the stem getting constricted due to space constraints in the net pot.

There's a general worry among hydroponic growers related to chemicals percolating from plastic into the hydroponic solution. For that reason, some hydroponic plastics are marked as 'food-grade'. The risk of chemicals percolating from plastic into the hydroponic solution is not unfounded, and it's always good to use the best quality of material. But don't be paranoid. Studies have established that the possibility of chemical percolation exists at high temperatures, but the chances of chemical percolation at low hydroponic temperatures are really low – unless someone uses a really cheap grade of plastic. It was already explained that DWC systems offer high volume-to-surface area – which also translates into lesser water coming in contact with the plastic - hence reducing the risk, if any, of chemicals percolating from plastic into the hydroponic solution. DWC reservoirs can even be made of metal if chemicals from plastic are to be avoided altogether and with certainty. But do not ever think of making them using cement or concrete – as these materials spoil the hydroponic solution by raising its pH.

Light damages the hydroponic solution as it causes algae to grow. That's why it's imperative to restrict the entry of sunlight rays in any kind of hydroponic system. In DWC systems, this risk is eliminated by the cover that shields the reservoir below it, ensuring that the growth of algae is not experienced even when the DWC systems are kept in direct sunlight for months on end.

Plant growth in hydroponic systems is much faster compared to normal soil-based cultivation – that's a known fact. On top of that, when arrangements are made to increase the span of light provided to plants, that further accelerates plant growth. When natural sunlight during the daytime is supplemented with indoor light systems to provide light during the nighttime, it's like making the plants work throughout the day – say 16 hours of direct light instead of 8 hours of sunlight – nearly doubling the growth rate. Coupled with the fact that hydroponic plants already grow faster than soil-based plants, achieving 4-5 times the growth rate of normal agriculture is possible. Stupendous!

DWC hydroponic systems are a good choice for a commercial hydroponics venture, without a doubt. Low-cost and high-performance.

There's another very popular type of hydroponics that falls within the fold of DWC hydroponics, which is practiced by hobby growers, and there's a high probability that the reader may have come across the word sometime. It's Kratky. It's only for hobby purposes.

Kratky Hydroponics

Kratky is a form of hydroponics that has been around for quite some time and popular with hobby hydroponists. It's <u>not</u> for commercial application. It's a simple, soil-free plant growing technique based on the DWC technique. The only difference between Kratky and DWC is that the Kratky technique does not use any air pump, and it operates without electricity, pumps, or water circulation. Kratky doesn't rely on external power sources. Rather, Kratky uses a very ingenious technique to naturally provide air to the roots.

Just like DWC, the plants are suspended above a container filled with nutrient-rich water. Plant roots are partly submerged in the nutrient solution, while the upper part of the plant sits inside the net pot on the cover. Part of the roots always remain exposed to air - that's where they pick up oxygen. That's the trick. Users just have to ensure that the roots are only partly submerged in the hydroponic solution and partly exposed to air. Daily visual checks become necessary. Plant growth in Kratky is not as spectacular due to limited air supply. Kratky is for beginners, more for ornamental type plants. Users may sometimes find it difficult to start it off from the sapling stage.

Recommendation is to practice DWC hydroponics straightaway, rather than taking the tortuous path via Kratky.

Nutrient management will be discussed separately and exclusively later, as it's common to all the hydroponic systems.

Let's summarize the benefits and drawbacks of DWC systems.

Benefits of DWC Systems:

High growth: DWC is a high-performance system, providing good yields and plant growth.

Versatile: Suits all plant types – small or big. This is the key differentiator as most other systems support only smallish plants. You can use both 2-inch and 3-inch net pots.

Reliable: DWC systems will keep working without any supervision and will continue to function well even if electrical power goes off for a long time.

Easy to assemble: DWC systems are quite easy to assemble, even for beginners. Unlike many other hydroponic systems, DWC systems can be easily made by oneself.

Scale up: DWC systems can be easily scaled up from hobby to commercial, using exactly the same principles.

Cost: DWC systems are low-cost, much lower in cost compared to many other hydroponic systems.

Low maintenance: DWC systems require very little maintenance and are very easy to clean and re-run. Just replenish the nutrient solution when needed and make sure your air pump is running. Nutrient solution management is easy.

No leakage: Since these systems do not use any pipes, channels, or joints, they do not have any leakage points.

Temperature Management: In outdoor hydroponics, DWC is better compared to other hydroponic systems in terms of keeping the hydroponic solution cool.

Drawbacks of DWC Systems:

DWC Hydroponics is not suitable for root plants like beetroot, radish, carrot, and potato.

DWC cannot be built as multi-story structures.

Beyond that, it's really hard to think of any limitations in the DWC systems.

A limitation could be that DWC systems do not look spectacular, meaning that they do not give an impression of having built something starkly different from conventional garden pots. At first glance, a casual person might not be able to readily distinguish that it's the hydroponic plants growing on top of the reservoir. That's until the cover/lid is lifted to expose the roots growing inside with air bubbling inside.

Here's a simple but very effective DWC hydroponic system that one can make at home, and the same approach can be expanded on a commercial scale.

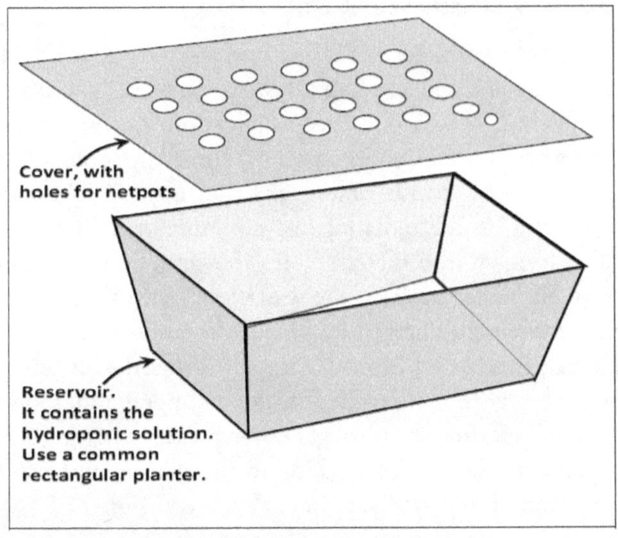

Cover, with holes for netpots
Reservoir. It contains the hydroponic solution. Use a common rectangular planter.

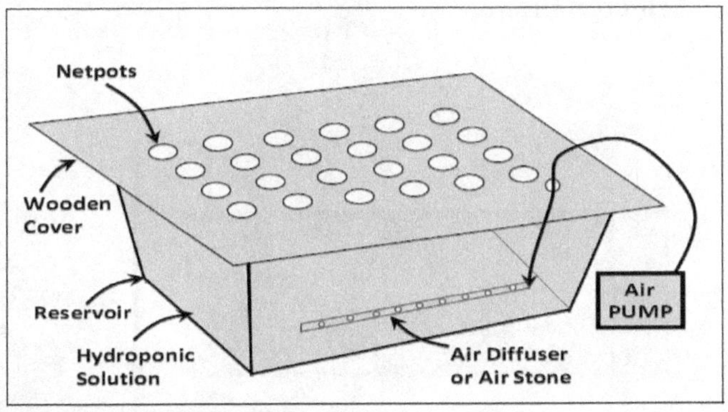

Netpots
Wooden Cover
Reservoir
Hydroponic Solution
Air Diffuser or Air Stone
Air PUMP

Flood and Drain (Ebb and Flow)

Armed with the knowledge of DWC systems, the reader would be able to grasp the Flood and Drain systems quite easily. Imagine a DWC system in which the submersible pump sitting inside the reservoir works intermittently to supply the hydroponic solution to net pots above - with time gaps. The supplied hydroponic solution drenches the roots for just a minute or 2, and then it drains back down into the reservoir. The cover of the system is located a bit higher up from the water level, such that the roots are not entirely submerged in the hydroponic solution. The benefit that is achieved from this design is that the air pump is avoided. The roots are drenched in the hydroponic solution for some time; thereafter, the roots get exposed to air with only a film of hydroponic solution left sticking to the roots. To switch the pump on and off repeatedly, a timer device is required.

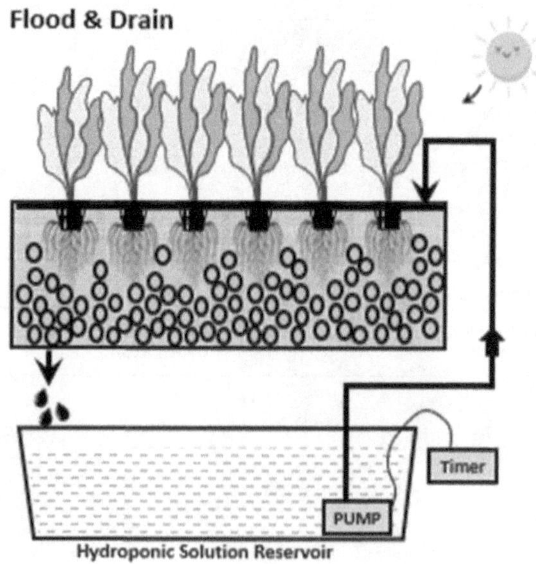

This is the concept, with many variations. Instead of having plants in net pots, it's common to use a growing bed that gets flooded by the nutrient solution from a reservoir below whenever the submersible pump in the reservoir starts through a timer. The pump stops when the timer stops, and the flooded bed gradually percolates by gravity to drain out the resident hydroponic solution into the reservoir below. If the reader would recall, this system is similar to the leachate collection system talked about in earlier Media Bed systems as well. During the stage when the growing bed is flooded, the plants consume the hydroponic solution through their roots. When the water drains and the grow bed empties, the roots get exposed to the air which helps in oxygenating the roots before the next flood comes in again by timer. Growers need to adjust the timing through their experience and depending upon the size of the growing bed, number & type of plants, and strength of the hydroponic solution used. Flood and Drain systems have benefits and drawbacks similar to those of DWC systems, except that they do not use an air pump but use a timer instead.

In case net pots are used, generally spray guns are installed close to the net pots that spray hydroponic solution on the roots – this arrangement becomes similar to an aeroponic system (covered later). Timing needs to be more frequent in such a system to prevent roots from drying out. In case a growing bed is made up of coco husk or cocopeat, water retention in the bed would be much longer lasting and the frequency of switching the water pump on/off will reduce considerably. LECA is also commonly used in the growing bed of such systems.

Flood and Drain systems can be used for almost every type of vegetable, even rooting plants like carrots, potatoes, beetroot, radishes, and the like. They can accommodate almost any type of vegetable. In case rooting plants are grown, the depth of the growing tray needs to increase considerably – making it unwieldy to accommodate above the reservoir and hence not common. Lettuce, strawberries, tomatoes, peas, beans, cucumbers, carrots, and peppers are popularly grown in these systems.

Benefits of Flood and Drain Systems:

Versatility:

- Flood and Drain hydroponic systems offer versatility, allowing one to grow larger plants as well as small plants compared to many other hydroponic methods.

- Suitable Crops: Fruits, flowers, and vegetables do well in these systems. When provided with an appropriately sized grow bed and proper nutrition, yields are good when timed/cycled correctly.

- The intermittent flooding and draining cycles provide air and nutrition.

DIY Set-up:

- Constructing Your Own System: Ebb and flow systems are DIY-friendly. It is not so difficult to assemble these systems using commonly available materials.

- While they may be slightly more expensive to set-up than simpler systems like wick or DWC, Flood and Drain systems accommodate a wide range of plant types.

Potential Drawbacks:

- Maintaining a well-functioning Flood and Drain system involves attention to detail and regular care. It's not really a fit-and-forget type.

- Pump Failure: Like any hydroponic system relying on a pump, Flood and Drain systems are vulnerable to pump malfunctions. Regular monitoring is needed.

- Sanitation and Maintenance: Proper hygiene is crucial. If the bed doesn't drain effectively, root diseases and rot can occur. A dirty system may also attract mold and insects.

- pH Fluctuations: Rapid changes in pH due to flooding and draining cycles may affect certain plants negatively.

Nutrient Film Technique

This is the most commonly sold hydroponic system.

Most commonly 'sold' system does not necessarily translate into being the best choice for a hydroponic system. Selling any product has a commercial driver that propels its marketing. NFT is promoted by equipment suppliers because it contains a lot of parts to sell and make a profit from.

NFT is an excellent system for small plants like Lettuce, Basil, Herbs, Spinach, and Strawberries, but it cannot cope with the demands of big plants like Tomatoes, Eggplants, Gourds, or vines. That's the crux, but it does not discount its importance or utility, especially as it offers multi-layered cultivation.

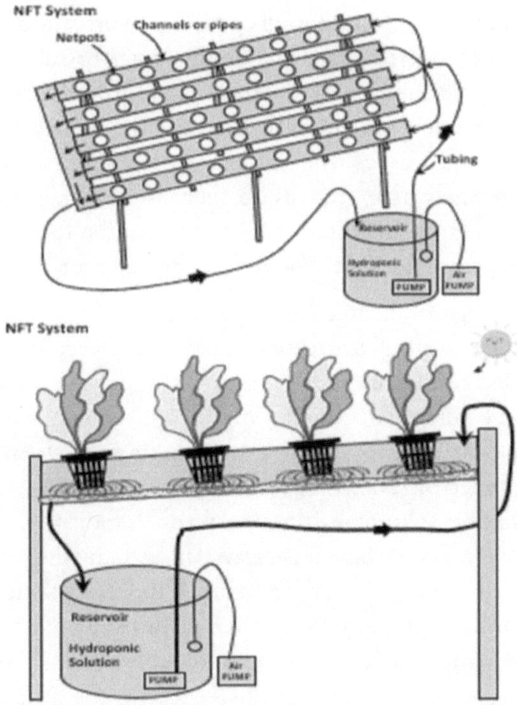

Nutrient Film Technique (NFT) comprises channels or pipes in which holes are drilled to accommodate the net pots. Nearly every NFT hydroponic system uses channels that are 2.5 inches high, and the most commonly used pipes in these systems are 3 inches in diameter. Net pots of 2-inch size can be accommodated in these channels or pipes, and the base of net pots comes very close to the channel bottom – just about a centimeter higher than the base of the channel. These channels are arranged in parallel and joined together using pipe fittings so that the hydroponic solution can enter from its one end and exit from the other end. The channel end where the hydroponic solution enters is a bit higher than the end from where it exits; the system is slightly tilted toward the exit points so that water can flow due to the gradient. The hydroponic solution hence creates a thin film inside the channels on the roots – that is where the NFT terminology comes from. This thin film of running hydroponic solution inside the channels (or pipes) and on the roots provides the water & nutrition required by the plants. The nutrient film created inside the channels continuously provides the nutrient solution that douses and washes over the plant's roots. Some advanced types of channels have grooves on their bottom side - to guide the shallow film of hydroponic solution over the root tips. This design prevents water from pooling against the roots.

This assemblage of channels or pipes is not self-supporting and requires some kind of structure to hold it in place. The support structure has to be sturdy enough to withstand the high winds, if it is used outdoors. Delivery of the hydroponic solution to the channels is done by using a water pump which sits inside a separate reservoir/tank that contains the hydroponic solution. The hydroponic solution exiting the channels returns back to the same reservoir, from where it is picked up again by the pump and delivered to the entry side of the channels through plastic tubing. Aeration of the hydroponic solution is achieved by putting an air pump inside the hydroponic solution tank.

To summarize and understand easily, here it is point by point:

In NFT systems, a film of continuously flowing stream of nutrient solution is maintained inside the channels.

Channels hold the plants and are tilted to allow the hydroponic solution to flow down its length.

Proper channel slope is crucial. Too steep, and water rushes down without nourishing the plants. Too much water flow can lead to overflow, and plant drowning.

The nutrient solution flows over the roots, creating a thin film.

The hydroponic solution drains into a reservoir located below the plants.

An air pump aerates the hydroponic solution in the tank.

A water pump recirculates the nutrient-rich hydroponic solution back to the top of the channels.

Roots in the channels are partly exposed to air inside the channels.

The exposed root system also has ample access to oxygen dissolved in the hydroponic solution.

The roots wick up moisture from this film, ensuring the plant receives nutrients.

Plant growth in NFT is good. Roots get drenched in the circulating nutrient solution that's running over the roots, causing a washing of roots. Washing of roots helps their growth.

The most important aspect in NFT is to continuously maintain the circulation of the hydroponic solution – from the reservoir via the pump to the channels and back to the reservoir. If the circulation stops, even for some time – like an hour or half, plants will be impacted. That's because the channels do not hold any liquid on their own due to the sloping. There is no accumulation of liquid in the channels. Liquid enters from the higher end and exits from the lower end – which means that if the circulating pump stops or malfunctions, then the plant roots will dry out and suffer. There have been instances when growers lost their entire production due to the pump malfunctioning in the middle of the night when nobody was awake. It's possible to add alarms that blare when the pump stops; this helps if someone's around and if a spare pump is readily available at hand to replace the malfunctioned pump.

NFT systems are significantly more expensive compared to DWC systems, as they involve using channels, pipes, tubing, fittings, and structure. Growers must consider their growing requirements before opting for these systems. The equipment suppliers would paint quite an enticing picture… understandably – which is correct in some parts and not so in others.

NFT systems are high-performance systems for small plants like lettuce, spinach, basil, pak choi, kale, herbs, and the like. Fruits like strawberries also do well. Plant growth is fast and meets expectations. However, for bigger plants, these systems do not remain useful as the roots of big plants like tomatoes, cucumber vines, gourds, etc., choke the channels. If the objective is to grow only small plants for perpetuity, NFT systems are a good choice.

It is easily possible to construct the NFT systems as a multi-story structure to save on real estate. This is a prominent benefit of the NFT technique, unlike DWC, which cannot be multi-story. When doing indoor hydroponics in greenhouses, this can become a significant factor in favor of NFT because the cost of constructing greenhouses is steep. Accommodating the maximum number of plants within the limited area of polyhouses is possible with NFT due to their multi-story construction possibility. While doing so, the grower has to ensure the availability of light to the plants from all angles at all growth stages, which sometimes becomes a challenge, obviating the gains derived through multi-story construction. Bigger plants also need a support mechanism to support the plants; otherwise, they will fall over – something that becomes difficult to achieve in multi-story construction.

Multi-storyed construction, while offering the benefits of maximum yield in the smallest floor area, comes with its own issues that the growers realize after installing them. How to access the plants located on the higher storys? The use of ladders becomes necessary, for which space provision needs to be made. Multistoryed constructions are inclined vertically, tapering toward the top. This makes the tapered top portions further away from the ladder and hence difficult to reach even with ladders. A person has to go up to access a part of the system, stretch over to reach the plants, then get down to move the ladder, and then climb up again. The labor involved in this is something that a person cannot visualize and appreciate prior to really getting into it.

NFT channels and pipes are not so easy to maintain. NFT channels are openable wherein the lid gets removed to access the portion inside. It's manageable in flat constructions, but imagine getting on to ladders to remove such lids in multi-storied construction! When pipes are used instead of channels for NFT systems, the growers realize later on that the pipes are impossible to clean unless they are dismantled in their entirety – an extremely undesirable situation.

Benefits of Nutrient Film Technique Systems

Low Water Consumption: NFT hydroponics recirculate the hydroponic solution, minimizing water usage – as in DWC also. A common NFT reservoir can supply the same hydroponic solution to a multitude of channel assemblies, helping in the consolidation of equipment. Using separate reservoirs for each set of channels is an extra investment but prevents total loss in case of pump failure or disease.

Due to the continuous flow of the hydroponic solution, there is a reduced risk of salt accumulation on plant roots.

Modular Design: NFT is commonly used in large-scale and commercial setups because there are numerous suppliers available to build them on order and supply as per one's specifications. NFT offers easy expansion. Once one set of channels is operational, growers get the hang of the system and keep adding more modules in parallel easily. Multiple modules in the same greenhouse can support different crops.

Drawbacks of NFT Systems:

Pump Failure: If the pump stops circulating the nutrient film, plants can dry out rapidly. This is the biggest risk that can occur. So, vigilance is essential to monitor pump performance.

Small plants: NFT is only for small plants, like lettuce. It's not meant for large plants, like tomatoes.

Overcrowding: Close plant spacing or excessive root growth can clog the channels. Obstructed channels prevent water flow, leading to plant starvation.

Uneven supply of hydroponic solution: The lower tier of the system can potentially receive more flow compared to the higher tiers. Uneven distribution impacts plant growth. Pay attention to plants at the top of the structure and consider adjustments if they underperform. NFT systems offer efficient nutrient delivery but require careful management.

Heat pickup: Due to the large, exposed surface area of the system by design, NFT systems tend to pick up more heat from the ambient air. That's why NFT systems are more suitable for hydroponics in indoor controlled environments.

Drip Systems

In a Drip hydroponic System, plants receive water and nutrients directly at their roots through a network of feeder lines and drips. This method offers precise control over the amount of moisture and nutrients plants receive, ensuring that they get exactly what they need to thrive.

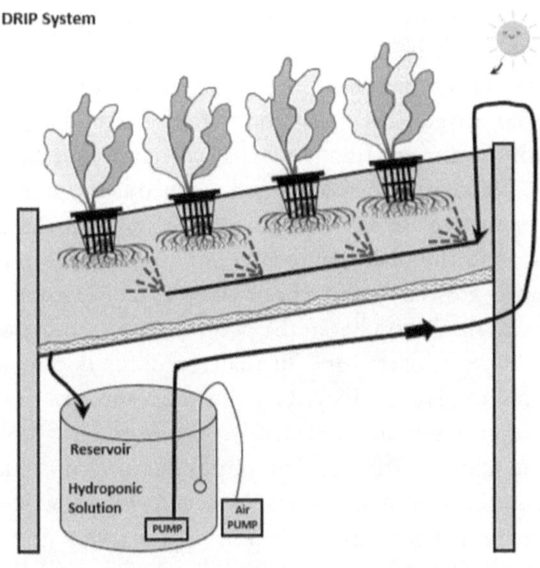

Drip hydroponic systems comprise a reservoir that contains a nutrient-rich hydroponic solution. A water pump circulates the hydroponic solution from the reservoir and supplies it to the plants via tubing. Tubing transports the water from the reservoir to individual plants. Drip Nozzles are small devices that are installed close to the plant roots and deliver the nutrient solution directly to the base of each plant. Drip systems are customizable and quite versatile. Drip systems can be customized to fit various settings ßnd plant types. Whether the person is growing a few plants at home or managing a large-scale commercial operation, drip systems can adapt to all needs.

There are 2 configurations of Drip System hydroponics: Recovery and Non-Recovery.

Recovery Systems: These are popular among at home growers. Excess water drains from the grow bed back into the reservoir, where it is re-circulated during the next drip cycle.

Non-Recovery Systems: More common among commercial growers. These systems allow excess water to drain out of the growing media and run to waste. It may sound wasteful that the nutrients are being sent to waste without circulating them. But large-scale growers have experience and are very conservative with water usage. They drip only a tiny amount per plant, minimizing wastage. This is where experience and fine-tuning come in. Elaborate timers and feeding schedules minimize waste by delivering precise amounts of solution to keep the growing media around the plant dampened. Still, one may wonder why commercial growers – for whom every penny matters – don't circulate it. The reason lies in the pH. In recovery systems, where wastewater recirculates, pH fluctuations occur due to nutrient depletion and plant activity. Growers must monitor and adjust the solution reservoir accordingly. However, by dosing the minimum amount, this problem of pH fluctuation is taken care of – though it requires considerable monitoring, experience, and care to achieve it properly. When using a recovery drip system, the grower will need to remain conscious of the pH levels and nutrient content to ensure healthy plant growth.

In the grow bed configuration, due to the constant dripping of the hydroponic solution at the same place in tiny amounts, the bed in the vicinity of the roots can get hyper-saturated with nutrients over time. Plants do not consume as many nutrients as they consume water, so remaining nutrients keep accumulating. For this reason, regular washing and replacement are necessary to maintain optimal conditions for plant growth. Drip nozzles also accumulate nutrients on their tip and can get clogged due to nutrient build-up over time. In general, drip systems provide efficient nutrient delivery while minimizing water waste, making them a popular choice for commercial hydroponics with deep pockets.

Benefits of Drip Systems:

Diverse planting options: Drip systems can support larger plants compared to NFT or Aeroponics. Commercial growers find them appealing for crops like melons, pumpkins, onions, and zucchinis. Drip systems accommodate larger root systems due to their ample growing media capacity. Slow-draining media (such as rockwool, coco coir, and peat moss) work well with drip systems.

Good Scalability: Drip systems are suitable for large-scale hydroponic operations. Adding more plants is straightforward: Connect new tubing to the reservoir and divert the solution. Existing drip systems can accommodate new crops by adding additional reservoirs with timers.

Drawbacks of Drip Systems:

Maintenance: Non-recovery drip systems at home require consistent monitoring of pH and nutrient levels. Regular draining and replacement becomes necessary. Debris and plant matter can clog delivery lines in recovery systems, necessitating regular cleaning and flushing.

Complexity: Drip systems can become intricate, especially in professional setups. For home growers, simpler systems like DWC are more ideal. Drip systems need proper management, crucial to avoid maintenance issues.

— ❖ —

Aeroponics

Aeroponics is what my nephew Kartik was referring to when he mentioned that plants can be grown in thin air!

Aeroponics is where the roots are suspended in air, receiving nutrients from a water-based solution delivered via a fine mist or spray. Plants are placed in net pots – held in place by anything that can hold them, from where the roots emerge and dangle in the air. Roots get covered with the nutrient solution that is being sprayed intermittently on them using special misting nozzles - in a fine mist form. The hydroponic solution from the reservoir is pumped to the spray nozzles, where the hydroponic solution is atomized and sprayed as a fine mist on root systems. Excess nutrient solution drips down into the collector to be re-circulated. The spray is not generally continuous, and the spraying action is controlled by a timer. This gives time for roots to absorb air between the spraying intervals. The timer is an essential component, but some aeroponic systems may continuously mist the plant's roots.

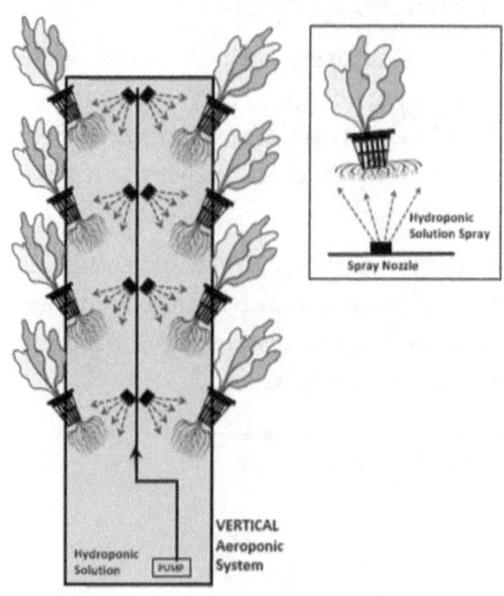

Aeroponic hydroponic systems are vertical towers or horizontal containers. Each enclosure holds the roots of a number of plants suspended from net pots arranged on the containers, or within net pots fixed to sides within the vertical towers. In horizontal setups, spray nozzles are located close to each plant's roots. In vertical systems, the spray nozzle is usually located at the top of the tower where mist is released, and it travels down the tower wetting the roots as it goes down in the chamber. In more advanced vertical systems, spray nozzles are located close to each plant's roots.

Aeroponic hydroponic systems do not require any substrate media as the roots' constant exposure to air and nutrient solution allows them to absorb water and take in oxygen, enabling them to grow at an accelerated rate.

Compared to all other hydroponic methods, aeroponics maximizes root exposure to oxygen, promoting rapid and healthy growth. This is the most advanced form of hydroponics, where the plant growth is maximized. Everything comes at a price. Aeroponic systems are the costliest to put together, most complicated, and most difficult to maintain. These are suited for experienced commercial growers with considerably deep pockets.

Following are the components of an aeroponics system:

Root Suspension: Plant roots are held in place by a frame at the top of an enclosure. Net pots secure the plants, allowing their roots to grow freely downward.

Chamber: An enclosed container that keeps out light and pests while maintaining humidity. Fresh air enters through open ports to ensure roots receive ample oxygen.

Nutrient Delivery: A nutrient solution is pumped from a reservoir through misters or sprayers at regular intervals. The fine mist nourishes the roots and prevents drying out.

No Growing Medium: Growing media such as perlite, LECA, or coconut coir are not required.

Aeroponic systems are extremely water-efficient. They consume a minimum amount of water compared to any other type of hydroponics. Studies have shown that water consumption in aeroponics is only around 5-10% of the water consumption in conventional soil-based agricultural methods. Aeroponic system design can be adapted to suit all sizes of plants – small or big, though they are usually used to grow expensive plants like lettuce, basil, baby greens, herbs, strawberries, etc. For big plants like tomatoes, bell peppers, eggplants, and vines, holding the large and heavy plant in place with roots dangling in the air becomes a daunting challenge – but theoretically possible. Rooting plants like potatoes, carrots, etc., are not generally grown in aeroponic systems, but it is possible.

Like all other forms of hydroponics, aeroponics allows for year-round growing in controlled atmospheres or in places where the climate remains naturally cool throughout the year. The possibility of erecting aeroponic systems as vertical structures makes them attractive where real estate is at a premium, as minimal space allows for the installation of a congregation of vertical towers. Providing light uniformly to them is key, and the grower needs to consider this. Climate-controlled greenhouses that are top-lit with sunlight are generally sufficient. Opaque spaces will need to have lots of artificial lighting all around the towers to make it possible to supply uniform light, making the arrangement unwieldy and cumbersome, apart from being super expensive.

Plant growth in aeroponics systems is the maximum out of all types of hydroponics, as the maximum surface area of roots is exposed to nutrients and air. When natural sunlight is supplemented with artificial light during the nighttime, plants grow even faster. It's like making the plants work double time or more, instead of 8 hours a day, so you can well imagine the phenomenal increase in growth.

Benefits of Aeroponic Systems:

Oxygen Maximization: Bare roots in aeroponic systems receive abundance of oxygen, promoting rapid plant growth.

Maximum water efficiency: Water consumption is the lowest among all methods of cultivation.

Modularization: Prefabricated aeroponic tower modules are available in the market to install straight away.

Transportability: Aeroponic systems can be easily moved without disrupting plant growth. During transportation, misting the roots prevents drying. Care has to be taken, though, to not dislodge the spray assemblies.

Ergonomics: Aeroponic Towers look out-of-this-world, creating an impression. These systems maximize space utilization and allow for denser plant growth.

Drawbacks of Aeroponic Systems:

Not DIY: These systems are difficult to make oneself and are better bought from expert manufacturers.

Small plants: Suitable for small plants with small root systems, but cannot be practically applied to big plants, such as tomatoes.

Expensive: Initial set-up costs for aeroponic systems are higher than for other hydroponic methods. A fully functional system with reservoirs, timers, and pumps can be costly.

Maintenance: Aeroponics systems require precise balance; disruptions can be fatal for plants.

Reliability: Failure of timers or pumps risks crop loss. Regular root chamber cleaning is required to prevent root diseases.

Requires expertise: Success in aeroponics demands technical expertise and experience. Proper care and attention are essential for optimal results.

Aquaponics

Aquaponics is the hydroponic method of growing plants, where the nutrients required by plants are provided by the excreta of fish. Aquaponics combines growing plants with growing fish. It's an integrated technique of growing plants using nutrients from fish excreta. In fact, aquaponics is more about pisciculture, i.e., the controlled breeding & rearing of fish, and less about growing plants. It primarily requires intricate knowledge of how the fish are bred and raised. Before going further, it's important to differentiate clearly between the 3 terminologies:

Pisciculture: This is the controlled breeding, growing & harvesting of fish.

Aquaculture: This is about breeding, growing, and harvesting several types of marine organisms like fish, shellfish, algae, etc.

Aquaponics: This is the breeding, growing, and harvesting of fish, integrated with the growing of plants.

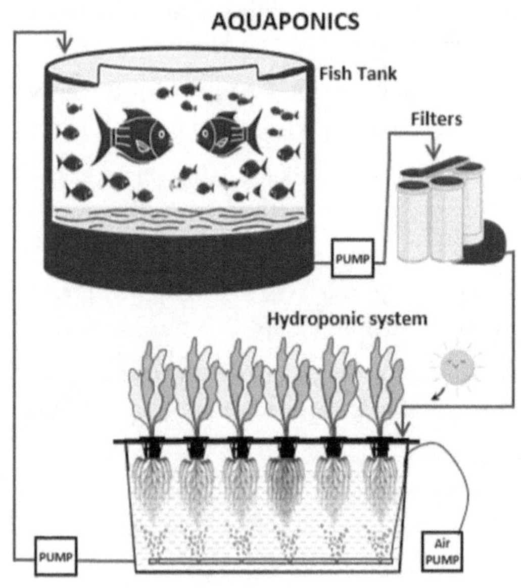

Aquaponics = hydroponics + Fish Farming.

Aquaponics uses any form of hydroponics, generally more suitable with DWC and NFT. An aquaculture system that recirculates water is known as a Recirculating Aquaculture System (RAS), which is often a contained system for fish farming that ensures the water remains clean through a filtration system. Although hydroponics and RAS can be successful and profitable on their own independently, there is an increasing fascination with aquaponics. It is said that a form of aquaponics existed even far back in the Mayan civilization in 1000 AD! How true... is difficult to ascertain.

In a basic aquaponic set-up, the nutrient-rich water from the fish tank passes through filters for the removal of solid particles and bio-filtration, then flows into the plant growth area before being re-circulated back into the fish tank. The removal of solid fish waste is an important part, and its design can be simple for small systems or automated for big systems. Bacteria are also a very important component of the aquaponic system. Bacteria are to be looked after and managed because bacteria present in the system convert ammonia and ammonium in the water to useful nitrates that can be picked by plants – thereby making these bacteria a crucial aspect of aquaponic systems. Plants absorb nitrates and other minerals from the recirculating filtered water that circulates between the fish tank and the plant growing area. In a harmonious symbiotic relationship, plants, fish, and bacteria all flourish. It's essential to manage all 3 components - fish, bacteria, and plants for the system to succeed.

Fish Section

The fish section is the tank where fish are kept in water and provided with food pellets for their breeding and growth. A common practice is to keep one kg of fish per 100 liters of water, which will vary depending on user experience, type of fish, and system design. Circular tanks are generally used for the purpose, made from materials like UV-resistant plastic or metal with a liner. The tank needs to have top protection in the form of a cover to prevent fish from leaping out, to prevent algae growth, and to prevent anything else from going in accidentally. Tilapia fish is popular in this context, though many types of fish are used such as hybrid striped bass, channel catfish, largemouth bass, bluegill, and hybrid sunfish. The survival and growth of fish require temperature control of the circulating water. Though it varies with the fish variety, generally, the water temperature needs to be maintained in a relatively narrow range between 15-25 degrees Celsius. It's costly to keep the water warm during winters. Heaters are used to maintain the temperature necessary for fish to live. Fish management is labor-intensive and time-consuming. They have to be observed daily, settled solids in the tank need to be siphoned off daily. As the waste generated would be biologically active waste, local municipal authorities may need to be checked with to dispose of it.

pH needs to be controlled as a continuous activity. A pH level between 5.5 to 9.0 is generally suitable for most fish, but for hydroponic plants, pH needs to be kept below 6.5. That's a contradiction that needs to be managed for the survival of both fish and plants. For that reason, maintaining pH between 5.5 to 6.5 becomes absolutely critical in aquaponics – which is a narrow range and hence requires constant supervision. The pH problem is compounded in aquaponics also because of the presence of microbes. Microbial activity of converting ammonia to nitrate keeps lowering the pH constantly. For that reason, pH control in aquaponics requires regular dosing of some external base supplement like potassium hydroxide that does not harm the fish.

Dissolved oxygen also needs to be monitored regularly. Dissolved oxygen levels above 5 ppm are ideal for fish, plants, and bacteria in the aquaponic system. Aeration of the tank is necessary using some sort of aeration pump that pulls in air and supplies it to the water in the tank through spargers. Fish need to be fed daily with the right amounts of solid pellet feeds. It's an involving activity.

Filter Section

Accumulation of fish waste and the remaining uneaten food needs constant attention, for which purpose the filtration unit becomes an essential part of aquaponics. Accumulation of this waste material will choke the system, leading to disruption of water flow and also lead to toxic conditions for fish. Filtration units comprising water clarifiers are available for this purpose. These units comprise an assembly of different types of filters – drum filter, bead filter, vortex filter, etc., supplemented by physical screens and solids settling tanks. For large systems, it makes sense to invest in automated filter units that free up labor and provide constancy of the filtration operation. For smaller systems, physical separation of solids by gravity settling and thereafter coupled with screens and baffles can be used.

Due to the presence of microbes, physical filtration is best augmented with bio-filtration in aquaponics, for which a Bio-filter is present where microbes convert ammonia to nitrite and then to nitrate. The size of the Bio-filter tank is generally a quarter of the volume of the fish tank. Biofilters are off-the-shelf products available in the market. They contain media that offers a large surface area for microbes/bacteria to colonize, with a good mechanism to provide aeration of the contents. Making one's own Bio-filter is also possible by assembling together any material that offers high surface area per volume – like cork, lava rock, or even packaging material, as long as it's inert and easy to clean.

Plant Section

Circulating filtered water from the filtration unit can now be directed to any hydroponic system like DWC or NFT as previously discussed. Aeroponics is avoided in aquaponics due to the propensity of the spray nozzles to get clogged because of the presence of organic matter.

It's important to select the plants for aquaponics, as the plant selection needs to match the fish in the tank. Both should have similar pH and temperature requirements. The kind of nutrients released by the fish should match the kind of nutrients required by the plants.

Commonly grown plants using the aquaponic technique are Lettuce, Herbs, Spinach, Basil, most kinds of leafy greens, pak choi, watercress, and Swiss chard. These plants can be grown completely relying on the nutrients provided by fish. However, fruiting plants would need to be provided with supplementary nutrition as the fish-based nutrition becomes insufficient for them. Fruiting plants like tomatoes, eggplants, cucumbers, gourds, and peppers fall into this category, requiring supplementary diet during the fruiting stage.

There are some nutrients that fish are generally not sufficient to fulfill, and deficiency of such gets manifested in the form of chlorosis, tip burn, blossom end rot, and yellow leaves. Hence, it's common for aquaponic systems to require supplementary addition of iron, potassium, and calcium. Each of these can be attended to through dosing of chelated iron, potassium hydroxide, and calcium hydroxide respectively.

This was an introduction to aquaponics. No book can be sufficient for learning aquaponics, as the pisciculture part requires one to learn it through direct experience only - by participating in live aquaponic farms.

--------◆◆--------

Indoor Vs Outdoor Hydroponics

Now that we are sufficiently knowledgeable about all types of hydroponics, there's one crucial aspect that should come next: Indoor vs. Outdoor forms of hydroponics.

All the types of hydroponics discussed can be practiced indoors as well as outdoors.

This is the key differentiator – make-or-break, for success and profitability of one's hydroponic venture.

Outdoor hydroponics is practiced out in the open, as the name suggests.

Outdoor hydroponics maximizes the usage of the free and naturally available key ingredient, namely, sunlight.

Light remains the basic prerequisite for any form of vegetation to grow, irrespective of how sophisticated a system one may install. When a hydroponic system is installed out in the open environment, it receives plenty of sunlight, for free. For that reason alone, outdoor hydroponics should be the way to go. But outdoor hydroponics comes with its own set of problems, with high temperature being the biggest of them. Direct exposure to sunlight causes the housing of hydroponic systems to get hot... very hot. It's called the Black body effect in scientific terms. One might recall how hot the car's dashboard gets when the car is left standing in the sun. Direct impingement of sunrays causes conductive surfaces like plastic to absorb a lot of heat, resulting in the car's dashboard getting as hot as 70 degrees Celsius even when the ambient air temperature might be less than 40 degrees Celsius. The Black body effect causes the hydroponic systems to get similarly hot when kept in direct sun. High temperature is the biggest enemy of hydroponics. To prevent high temperature in outdoor systems, the body of the hydroponic systems should be shaded when kept outdoors, to prevent direct sunlight from falling upon their surface. Shading the hydroponic system from the sun helps to a fair extent, but the problem does not end there.

Another problem in outdoor hydroponic systems is the hot air of the summer months. When the ambient air temperature is more than 35 degrees Celsius, hydroponic plants lose a lot of water through transpiration from their leaves. This leads to aggravated depletion of water from the hydroponic solution, requiring its frequent replenishment that takes its toll - by way of pH fluctuation and build-up of hardness from topped up water. Every time water is topped up into the hydroponic solution, it carries along its own water hardness that serves to gradually raise the TDS of the hydroponic solution. Outdoor hydroponics is feasible but in regions where summers are not too harsh, or in months when the air is not very hot.

Also, hydroponic plants do not have a strong foothold, owing to the fact that their roots are suspended in water or air. Their roots are not grounded firmly as in soil plants. Strong winds or heavy rain can dislodge the hydroponic plants in outdoor hydroponic setups despite supporting them through trellis arrangements.

Indoor hydroponics is free from all these perils of hot incident sun, hot air, strong breeze, and rain. Indoor hydroponics is practiced in climate-controlled environments inside polyhouses where air temperature is controlled, and the polyhouse provides protection from the natural forces. Sunlight filters through the polyhouse and can be sufficient to grow plants or can be supplemented by installing indoor grow lights. A climate-controlled environment and artificial lighting require a significant investment but allow the grower uninterrupted growing throughout the year. Apart from the high investment cost, the only other issue indoor hydroponics faces is that natural pollination of flowers is missing indoors. That's because the bees required to do flower pollination cannot find their way inside closed polyhouses. For that reason, indoor hydroponics is generally practiced for leafy greens that are not flowering and hence do not require pollination. When growing flowering plants like tomatoes indoors, growers have to resort to doing pollination manually using a brush or shaking the plants or likewise – that can be really bothersome but has to be done.

In my experience, basements of houses can be perfect for practicing indoor hydroponics. Basements are generally cooler owing to the fact that they are shielded from direct sun. We have successfully managed to grow basil, lettuce, and pak choi in basements using indoor grow lights – without any kind of climate control or air-conditioning - despite searing hot temperatures of 45 degrees C outside in the open in the north of India.

For hobby enthusiasts, growing veggies round the year inside their own houses using indoor grow lights is very much possible, depending upon the air temperature they can maintain inside their houses. Inside the house is generally cooler compared to the hot sun outside, even in hot summers. Practicing outdoor hydroponics in winters is without question the preferred way to go, as long as the winter does not become too severe with air temperatures dropping below 6 degrees Celsius – in which case just adding a small heater to the hydroponic solution tank suffices to maintain its temperature above 6 degrees Celsius. Note that there is no need to heat the entire ambiance around the hydroponic system in extreme winters; just heating the hydroponic solution slightly does the trick.

For professional growers, indoor hydroponics with a polyhouse is the way to go in regions where temperatures can get quite hot. In case the professional grower is fortunate to be located in a part of the world where summers are not extreme, they can do with outdoor hydroponics easily to save on the cost.

———•••———

Chapter 4

Hydroponic Elements

TDS (Total Dissolved Solids), EC

She was in the second grade of her schooling when my niece Saesha made a YouTube video on how to prepare lemonade… *Shikanji*. It's a fascinating watch, with her tiny tot imparting instructions on how much salt and sugar to add to water and then for how long to stir the solution to ensure it's all dissolved.

Salt and sugar are solids that dissolve when added to water to become 'Dissolved Solids' or TDS.

TDS = Total Dissolved Solids.

The concept of TDS is as simple as that, yet it is the most important parameter to look out for in hydroponics.

TDS of any solution tells how many salts are dissolved in that solution.

Without realizing it, that is what little Saesha was telling the audience – how much TDS to maintain in the lemonade using salt and sugar.

Similarly, TDS of the hydroponic solution tells how much hydroponic nutrients are dissolved in that hydroponic solution.

But there's a catch.

Water has hardness – everyone knows.

The more dissolved solids in water, the higher its hardness.

Distilled Water (used in car batteries) has TDS = ZERO, meaning no solids.

Bottled drinking water typically has a TDS of 50-100.

River water typically has a TDS of 100-150. When (& if) supplied, river water is usually the municipal water supplied by the government to homes.

Sea water's TDS is more than 10,000.

The Dead Sea has the saltiest water on Earth – with a Total Dissolved Solids (TDS) level of more than 300,000! It's the best place for any non-swimmer to learn swimming – the person will simply float effortlessly. The only issue is that the person will get dehydrated if they stay in there for long. That's because of leaching – bodily fluids will tend to leach out into the external hypertonic environment.

TDS of groundwater varies considerably depending on location. Typically, the TDS of groundwater is high, in the range of 300–700.

My close friend Ritesh hails from Agra, and the TDS discussion irks him. Groundwater in several parts of Agra has very high levels at 2000-3000 TDS. Brushing teeth with it leaves a salty aftertaste. Bathroom fittings corrode away fast. Soap does not generate lather in such high saline water – how to bathe! Utensils have a perpetual white layer of calcium precipitate. Living in Agra is not easy. Empathize, but never discuss water with a person from Agra.

That's why RO filters have become essential in every urban household these days.

RO filters reduce the hardness of water by removing its dissolved salt content.

To an extent, dissolved salts in water are beneficial for the human body.

But humans are an over-zealous race and overdo everything.

The vast majority of RO filters remove nearly all the dissolved salts from water. The resulting water becomes super-soft and devoid of any salt content. Such super-soft water enters the human body and has a tendency to 'pick up' salts & nutrients from the human body. That's the sponge effect. A dry sponge is devoid of water, so it has the propensity to pick up water from its surroundings. That's nature's balancing act. Nature always tries to bring everything to an equilibrium stable state.

Just like a dry sponge absorbs water because it does not have any water on itself, super-soft water is attracted to salts because it does not have any salts with itself. Super-soft water picks up salts from inside our own body. That's a loss. That's the terrible leaching effect, because of losing the bodily nutrients into water and out of the body. Please, never drink super-soft water, and ensure your drinking water has some hardness in it – say 200-300 TDS for it to be healthy. There used to be an earlier guideline from WHO recommending drinking water to have up to 300 TDS; recently, that guideline has gone, and there's no WHO limit as such on TDS.

The foregoing discussion was necessary to understand the concept where it matters.

A feeling of the concept is important to be able to visualize its impact.

This book attempts to understand the concepts in a practical manner from everyday life and apply them gradually and logically on the path to a hydroponic Life.

Before delving into details, we were discussing the following:

TDS of the hydroponic solution tells us how many hydroponic nutrients are dissolved in that hydroponic solution.

And there's an important catch.

Water used to make the hydroponic solution, by itself, has hardness in it, which the reader would well appreciate by now through the preceding discussion. It's also now understood that some hardness in water is good and important for human bodies. But for hydroponics, the hardness of water is BAD, in any measure. While human bodies make use of the water hardness, plants cannot use the water hardness. It would need a lot of chemistry to understand why such a big difference exists. Chemistry doesn't excite anyone generally. Here, the attempt is to avoid theory as much as possible; this is not a theory book. So, we will entirely side-step the discussion of why water hardness is fine for human bodies but BAD for plants and just get on with an incredibly interesting discussion by taking it for a fact – that water hardness is BAD in hydroponics.

Water hardness has ruined the profitability of many a commercial hydroponic plant, halting their operations.

Water hardness can determine whether or not hydroponics can be performed.

Alas! The importance due to water hardness is never given its due by contemporary hydroponic gurus, online classes, product literature & the like. But this single parameter will decide the viability of the hydroponic project.

It's so important and so interesting; hence, that's what will be discussed gradually hereafter to understand it completely. That's the intention of this book – to unravel what is really important toward successful hydroponics.

Some may argue - everything is important. True, everything is important. Like in life, everything is important. But then, something has to be more important than the other. Focusing energy on everything is possible, but difficult. Focusing is a narrowing down exercise. Focus means to view a target-specific area – which is selected due to its relative importance. In life, especially professional lives, we come across considerable contradictions. Haven't we all heard in our professional lives' adages like 'let's look at all aspects', 'let's cover all angles', 'let's be focused', 'let's target' etc.? Can anyone ever be comprehensive as well as be targeted? Adages are good to throw at people, but with limited utility, so let's continue with our hydroponic Bliss.

It's understood thus far that:

TDS of the hydroponic solution tells us how much hydroponic nutrients are dissolved in that hydroponic solution.

There's a catch.

Water hardness is bad in hydroponics.

Because water hardness is high in hydroponics, should it be removed entirely? YES, please do.

But the problem is that removing water's hardness is expensive. Quite expensive. It consumes electricity, and it also generates unusable reject wastewater.

Plants will continue to consume water during their entire life, and that will require continuously topping up water in the hydroponic systems – to compensate for the water lost through transpiration of leaves and possible evaporation. Over the entire life cycle of plants, there may be a considerable amount of water that would need to be topped up. So, while it's important to remove the water hardness, it also makes business sense to tolerate it somehow if possible. We'll learn to do that exactly, and to understand that some minimum maths becomes necessary… my apologies.

TDS of the hydroponic solution =

TDS added due to the addition of nutrients + TDS due to the hardness of water.

Let's explain by using our own GreenLoop Hydroponic Nutrients to illustrate the concept.

1 ml of each stock A & B (of GreenLoop LEAFY-200 nutrients) when added to 1 liter of water, adds TDS of 117 to the water.

To make the hydroponic solution, GreenLoop recommends adding 5 ml of each stock solution per liter of water taken.

In this example, let's use soft water (TDS = 50).

By adding 5 ml of each Stock A and B per liter of water,

Hydroponic solution TDS = 50 + 5*117 = 535.

Here, the total TDS becomes only 535.

For most leafy vegetables, the acceptable maximum TDS is approximately 1500.

That means there's room to add more nutrients in the solution, if needed.

Even if we double the nutrient dosing to 10 ml of Stock A+B per liter,

Hydroponic solution TDS = 50 + 10*117 = 1220.

As evident here, the total TDS of 1220 is still less than the maximum acceptable TDS of 1500. Still OK.

In this same example above, what would happen if hard water were used?

Try using hard water (TDS = 600).

By adding 5 ml of each stock A and B per liter of water, the hydroponic solution TDS is calculated as 600 + 5*117 = 1185.

As can be seen here, the total TDS is already 1185 – quite close to the acceptable maximum TDS of 1500 for most leafy vegetables, leaving little room for adding more nutrients.

What has been learned?

By using soft water, it becomes possible to add in more nutrients to the same hydroponic solution.

This can be better for the improved growth of plants during the fruiting stage.

Also, prevents nutrient deficiency in the solution.

It also allows the grower to relax, as there is now no need to worry about topping up nutrients too often.

Soft water also allows more buffer in the hydroponic solution to accommodate a gradual increase in TDS that will happen due to regular additions of top-up water, meaning the same hydroponic solution can last longer.

Above is sufficient learning to understand the next part, which is to understand how some water hardness can be tolerated because it's expensive to remove hardness, and business sense requires tolerating some of the water hardness.

It is evident from the preceding examples that it is possible to accommodate some water hardness, but not too much.

If water with high TDS is used, it means the hydroponic solution has a lesser capacity to accommodate nutrients.

By using soft water, the same nutrient solution can be used for a longer time. Hard water can also be used, but it will require more frequent replacement of nutrients. Plants would grow faster if soft water were used.

Removing all the water hardness would be prohibitively expensive.

Tolerating, say, 100–150 ppm of water hardness would still allow sufficient room to top-up nutrients liberally and allow longevity of the nutrient solution at the same time.

As the water gets evaporated due to topping up, additional water hardness would get added to the hydroponic solution every time water is topped up. So, there needs to be a mechanism for the grower to be able to predict how much useful hardness remains in the hydroponic solution due to nutrients, and how much useless hardness is present due to water hardness. This is really difficult.

Where GreenLoop Hydroponic Nutrients are used, the company provides a free mobile app and Excel calculator to its users, using which users can get this analysis on a real-time basis, for free. This becomes possible as the GreenLoop Nutrients are calibrated, which means the users would know exactly by how much the TDS will increase due to adding how much of these nutrients. The mobile phone app can be downloaded on one's phone from Play Store and it's remarkably versatile and easy to use – the only such app in India, maybe the world. GreenLoop hydroponic nutrient Calculator also comes in the form of an Excel spreadsheet. This calculator file/app allows users to know exactly how many useful nutrients and how much useless hardness remains in the solution, and how much nutrient to top-up, by doing a very simple TDS measurement. That's the kind of ease that the users need. This information is essential for any kind of predictive analysis. Users do not need to be bombarded with esoteric scientific terminologies and don't want to become scientists in their pursuit of a healthy hydroponic venture. But if someone is making their own nutrient mix, it would not be possible to predict how much useful hardness remains due to nutrients, and how much useless hardness is present due to water hardness.

If a person is doing small-scale hobby hydroponics, it is possible to use hard water even with a TDS of 500. But that will require changing the hydroponic solution more often as the solution's TDS will exceed 1500 much sooner compared to when soft water was used instead.

If the intent is to get into professional large-scale hydroponic setups, it would make sense to reduce the expenditure of water hardness removal. That objective can be achieved through 2 ways. First, select the location of the plant set-up close to a river water source so that low TDS water at 100-150 ppm becomes available without having to spend any extra money. Second, even if the person is not close to a river, ensure that municipal water supply is available in the locality and make arrangements to store it. Municipal water is sourced from river water and generally has low TDS.

There's one more concept related to TDS in hydroponics that needs to be understood and appreciated.

As the plants grow, they consume nutrients. The hydroponic solution has a mixture of nutrients – salts of calcium, nitrogen, potassium, phosphate, sulfur, carbon, iron, and important micronutrients. Different plants consume these nutrients differently – depending on their own requirements. Some plants consume calcium more, while others may consume nitrogen more. These consumptions also vary depending on the growth stage of the plant. During the fruiting stage, for example, tomatoes consume calcium more. After some time, the hydroponic solution will get richer in those nutrients that are least consumed by plants, and it will get leaner in those nutrients that the plants consume the most. It is practically impossible to tell which nutrients are how much in the hydroponic solution at any point in time. It is possible if very expensive online analytical instruments & techniques are utilized, but to the best of available knowledge, not even large commercial setups can afford these. Again, this is something that will not be told by any hydroponic guru or class. This is the part that will always remain unknown. So, what to do? The best insurance against this is as follows:

1. Maintain a large volume of hydroponic solution per plant. This will be covered in detail in a later chapter.

2. Keep adding nutrients regularly in small doses so that the nutrients that plants need are always available, even if the solution is rich in not-so-needed nutrients.

3. Use soft water so that the hydroponic solution has the capacity to hold more nutrients, as explained earlier.

4. Change the hydroponic solution entirely after approximately 12-14 weeks of usage – if soft water is being used with TDS < 100. If hard water is being used, that will require changing earlier. The GreenLoop App tells you that too.

All that was necessary to know about TDS is now known.

Except for the measurement of TDS.

TDS of a hydroponic solution can be measured easily using a simple TDS meter. It's a cheap device easily available in online stores. There are 2 problems associated with TDS meters.

Firstly, most TDS meters are configured to measure the TDS of plain water. For this reason, they give accurate readings in the low range of measurement, but not necessarily in the higher range. Since they are configured for water, these are generally 3-digit meters, meaning they will measure up to 999 only. For hydroponics, it's always better to buy a TDS meter that has 4 digits and calibrate it using the calibration salts generally provided in the package by good suppliers.

Two different TDS meters give different readings in the same solution. See the image of 3 different pH meters when put in the same hydroponic solution, and as is evident, all 3 show different readings. To tackle this problem, the user should use the same TDS meter for repeated readings, and that will take care of the zero error in the TDS meter.

GreenLoop Nutrient Calculator app automatically takes care of this aspect as well.

912
825
494
TDS
TDS&EC

EC (Electrical Conductivity)

EC (Electrical Conductivity) is a topic that manages to confuse most hydroponic enthusiasts. EC is the measure of the amount of dissolved minerals in the hydroponic solution and is measured in millisiemens per centimeter (mS/cm).

Wait a minute, isn't that what the TDS also tells – the amount of dissolved minerals in the hydroponic solution? Yes, of course. Then what's the difference?

Theoretically, there's a wee bit of difference. TDS is a measure of dissolved minerals, while EC takes into account anything else that might be mixed in the solution, like dissolved gases. But the point here is, there is nothing else added in the hydroponic solution other than the minerals. So, for the purpose of hydroponics, TDS and EC are safely and easily interchangeable, using a conversion factor. There is no need for a hydroponic grower to invest money and time in taking EC readings. Every measurement meter comes with its own zero error... inaccuracy, and there is no need to confuse oneself by taking EC readings simultaneously with TDS readings. Just rely on TDS readings, and that's sufficient.

Still, if the hydroponic really needs to know the EC of the hydroponic solution, just divide TDS by 500, and that's your EC in milliSiemens/cm. That's easy.

⚬⚬

pH

pH is the measure of the acidity or alkalinity of a solution.

pH value tells whether the solution is acidic or alkaline (basic).

Technically, pH is the measure of hydrogen ion concentration in a solution. Without getting into its technicalities, the discussion will be restricted to pH for hydroponic applications only.

The pH scale is between 0 and 14.

Values less than 7 are acidic, and values more than 7 are alkaline (basic).

Value 7 is Neutral.

It's common to hear people say… let's use pH DOWN. What does it mean?

When the pH of a solution is going up, it means the pH value is increasing.

When the pH of a solution is going DOWN, it means the pH value is decreasing.

When pH is rising, it needs to be reduced by adding pH DOWN solution.

When pH is going DOWN, it needs to be increased by adding pH UP solution.

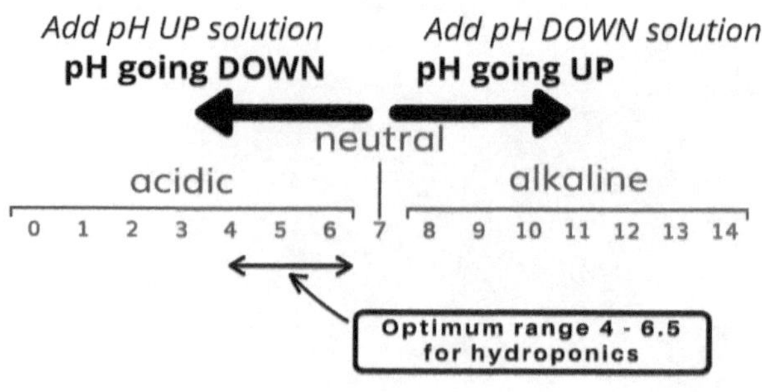

OK, now with that understanding, it's time to go deeper.

For hydroponics, the best pH range is between 5.5 and 6.5.

Note that this is the 'Best' range, but plants remain OK even if the range gets exceeded somewhat.

The optimum working range of pH is 4 to 6.5, even up to 7.

Beyond this range of 4–6.5, the user needs to take corrective action to rectify the hydroponic solution.

Deviation toward the acidic side (low pH) is actually not much of an issue. Hydroponic plants like an acidic medium, and you can operate hydroponic systems for extended periods of time with a pH as low as 3.5.

Deviation toward the alkaline (basic) side, beyond 6.5, is surely a problem.

It should also be understood what happens beyond the recommended pH range.

Too acidic (Low pH... less than 4) or too alkaline (high pH... more than 6.5) leads to 'nutrient lock-out' – which means roots are not able to pick up nutrients even though nutrients are present in the nutrient solution. When this happens, leaves will start showing all kinds of symptoms of nutrient deficiency, and plant growth will reduce.

High pH also leads to another very significant problem, and that is nutrient precipitation. This means the nutrients will start dropping out of the solution as solid, insoluble matter and deposit onto the surface of the hydroponic system. Most commonly, these appear as a white, crystalline layer deposited on the surface. These precipitated nutrients are a loss – not only in the form of losing valuable nutrients but also because these nutrients do not become available for plant growth. That's not good.

Given all the issues that were discussed regarding pH, naturally one's thoughts would be to control the pH as much as possible within the recommended range.

Here again, the recommendation is to take it easy. Relax. There's no need to go all guns blazing to control the pH within the range through hourly or daily pH measurements.

pH does not change suddenly. It's not that if the pH is 6 right now, it will become 8 after a few hours. No, that will not happen. pH always changes gradually and slowly. When the users take the pH readings in their own hydroponic system a few times, they will automatically get a fair idea of how fast the pH is drifting. pH drift will gradually slow down over time, which means it will initially drift at a faster pace and gradually the pace of its drifting will slow down… it'll be good to understand this.

That's because pH is not linear.

pH is not linear, but exponential.

That's the reason why the user will not be able to predict the speed at which the pH will increase. The user might think that he/she will be able to predict where the pH will go after a certain duration, but sorry – that will most likely not be a successful attempt because pH change is exponential and not linear.

If the solution takes some effort to go from pH 4 to 5, then it will take 10 times the effort to go from 5 to 6.

To put it more technically, if it takes 5 hydrogen ions to increase the pH from 4 to 5, then it will take 10 x 5 = 50 hydrogen ions to go from 5 to 6.

This is important to understand, as this tells us that every next increment of pH will take 10 times more time or effort compared to the earlier increment.

If pH took 1 hour to go up from 4 to 5, it might take 10 hours to go up from 5 to 6, and then it may take 100 hours to go up from 6 to 7, approximately.

Now you must have understood why you were asked to relax and not get too paranoid about taking frequent pH readings. As the pH rises, it takes much more time to increase.

Now, let's discuss more specifically.

<u>Problem of pH going DOWN (meaning going below 4).</u>

In hydroponics, the pH of the hydroponic solution does NOT generally have the tendency to go down (to a lesser value). This means it does not become more acidic over time. Instead, it will generally become more alkaline (basic) over time.

So, pH going DOWN is not much of an issue in hydroponics, unless the user is using highly acidic water.

Baking soda may be used to increase pH, but it adds sodium to the hydroponic solution.

The use of commercially available pH UP solution is recommended.

<u>Problem of pH going UP (meaning going above 6.5).</u>

In hydroponics, the pH of the hydroponic solution generally tends to increase (go up) over time, which means it becomes more alkaline (basic) over time and continues to rise above 6.5.

Higher pH leads to the precipitation of calcium, potassium, magnesium, and, most importantly, micronutrients like iron.

pH of the hydroponic solution will also increase over time as the TDS increases. An increase in TDS raises the pH.

There are several ways of reducing the pH.

Addition of strong acids (like Nitric Acid, Sulfuric Acid, Hydrochloric Acid) is practiced by experts. However, these acids are difficult to handle, can corrode, may fume, and are dangerous to handle. Unless you are an expert, this is NOT recommended.

Citric Acid or Vinegar is a choice, but these are weak acids and give only a short-term pH reduction. Use them, and in a few hours, the pH will go back to where it was.

Ammonium nitrate, phosphoric acid, ammonium phosphate, urea phosphate, phosphoric acid, and EDTA are good choices, but impact the composition of the hydroponic solution.

Commercially available pH down solutions are most recommended for this purpose, especially for hobby users.

Whatever you use, make sure it's not dangerous, gives long-term pH correction and does not unduly impact the

The addition of hydroponic nutrients also reduces pH slightly.

Oxygenating the hydroponic solution also brings down its pH temporarily, as long as high oxygen remains.

A point to add here is that some foreign hydroponic nutrient makers use special micronutrients that remain stable at all practical pH ranges of hydroponic solutions. These micronutrients are extra expensive and are not normally used in usual commercially available micronutrient mixtures. In India, GreenLoop uses such micronutrients.

Let's also understand what causes the increase in pH.

Roots of most plants tend to turn the hydroponic solution more alkaline as they grow. Take tomatoes, for instance; their plant roots are notorious for increasing the pH quite frequently, and hence the grower needs to keep an eye on pH while growing tomatoes. However, when growing small plants like lettuce and spinach, the rate of increase in pH is not as high.

While using the same hydroponic solution for a long time, a grower would observe that the pH will generally increase after a few weeks. Some growers recommend that changing the nutrient solution entirely is a good insurance.

Using hard water also increases the pH.

<u>Short recap of pH in hydroponics:</u>

Keep the pH in the range of 4 to 6.5.

The pH of the hydroponic solution normally increases over time. The rate of increase decreases over time.

Use pH DOWN solution to lower the pH.

No need to be paranoid over pH monitoring.

Checking pH is important if:

- hard water is being used, and/or,

- the same hydroponic solution is being used for long durations, and/or

- if plants with big root systems are being grown.

Humidity

Humidity is an important factor to be considered in hydroponics. Humidity is the measure of water vapor present in the air. Most plants thrive in relatively high humidity in the range of 50-70% relative humidity. Some plants like cantaloupe, cucumber, and zucchini thrive in even higher humidity. But if the air is too dry, as in low-humidity conditions, that leads to higher transpiration losses through the leaf surfaces, which the plants will have to make up by pulling more water from the hydroponic solution. Along with the increased rate of water uptake, the uptake of nutrients will also increase – as both come from the same hydroponic solution – leading to risks of nutrient toxicity. Plants may not be able to continuously uptake the increased water amount to cope with the increased transpiration loss, thereby leading to wilting of plants.

Though high humidity is a lesser problem compared to low-humidity, it too needs to be managed. High humidity can lead to the growth of fungi, resulting in rot, mold, and mildew problems. High humidity will also cause the ambiance to get warmer. If the reader recalls from the climate section, it was discussed that water vapor is 4 times more effective in retaining heat compared to carbon dioxide, a common greenhouse gas. High humidity also restricts the plants' ability to respire, as the plant's transpiration decreases, affecting plant metabolism.

For successful hydroponics, it's good to manage humidity effectively.

When practicing outdoor hydroponics, humidity is not possible to control, as it is what is there in the environment. In situations of low-humidity environments, occasionally misting the plants with water can help for outdoor hydroponic systems. But beyond that, there is a limitation in outdoor hydroponics. Humidity can be well controlled in indoor hydroponics, like in polyhouses – a considerable benefit and insurance against a failed crop due to the climate turning.

Actually, a hydroponic system when kept indoors becomes an automatic natural humidifier for the ambiance! That's because the plants lose water through transpiration, with that water vapor serving to humidify the ambiance. This can be particularly useful for residential homes in winters when the atmospheric humidity is low. When the air is far too dry, it leads to various respiratory problems and colds.

Air temperature and humidity go hand in hand. The higher the air temperature, the more would be the water vapor handling capacity of the air. Air conditioners reduce air temperature, thereby reducing the moisture in the air – reducing humidity. The atmosphere inside the airplanes is as dry as a desert for that reason. Reducing air temperature is the only practical method to reduce air humidity, requiring the installation of air conditioners. Another method is to use water-absorbing media like silica gel – but that's impractical and way too expensive. How long can anyone keep using and regenerating silica gel? To reduce humidity inside the commercial polyhouses, growers prefer not to use either of these approaches. Instead, commercial growers reduce the humidity inside polyhouses as much as possible through air circulation only and by venting out the moisture-laden air. Humidistats are commonly used for this purpose in commercial polyhouses. Humidistats are controllers that regulate humidity levels in a closed environment. These devices monitor the moisture content in the air. As and when the humidity goes beyond the upper limit of the desirable range, humidistats switch on the ventilation systems comprising of fans and simultaneously open the ventilation doors. It is rare to encounter a low-humidity situation inside polyhouses because the plants are continuously releasing water vapor into the ambiance.

———◆◆———

Temperature

About the importance of temperature in hydroponics, much has already been explained while explaining various kinds of hydroponic systems. For a reader who skipped, it's explained briefly below, with some additional information.

When talking about temperature, it's important to differentiate which temperature is being referred to – the temperature of the 'Hydroponic Solution' or the temperature of the 'Air'. Both are important.

Temperature of the 'Hydroponic Solution' is important due to 2 reasons. At high temperatures of the hydroponic solution, uptake of water and nutrients gets adversely impacted. The higher the temperature, the lesser the water and nutrient pickup by roots, which can be fatal for plants. Due to this reason, the temperature of the hydroponic solution should remain in the range of 8-20 degrees Celsius. Up to 25 degrees Celsius is also OK, but when it crosses 30 degrees Celsius, the uptake is severely impacted. The second reason is that the oxygen saturation capacity of water reduces as its temperature increases. The solubility of oxygen in water nearly doubles at 10 degrees Celsius compared to 30 degrees Celsius. Even if the air is being bubbled into the solution at full throttle, it would not be retained in water when the water temperature is high. Oxygen is essential for roots, in the absence of which the roots rot. Solution temperatures need to be maintained between 8-25 degrees Celsius for best performance. Lesser temperatures down to 6 degrees Celsius are also tolerated, but temperatures lower than that need to be prevented by the installation of a simple water heater.

All plants need a suitable temperature range of air to thrive as per their natural constitution. Some plants thrive in cold air, while some do well in warm air. Plant-wise natural requirements of air temperature have to be provided for the plant to grow. Air temperature is also important as it directly impacts the transpiration process from the leaves of the plant. In summer months, the air temperature goes really high, as everyone knows. When the ambient air temperature is more than 30-35 degrees Celsius, hydroponic plants lose a lot of water through transpiration from their leaves. To make up for that water loss, plants try their best to pull water through their root systems but get stressed in the process. The hydroponic solution also gets depleted fast, requiring its frequent replenishment. Water hardness starts building faster. As plants drink more water from the hydroponic solution, they end up drinking more nutrients as well from the same solution, leading to nutrient toxicity. Leaf quality and texture at high air temperatures also get impacted.

Air temperature and humidity are also related. Air holds more water vapor at elevated temperatures. The air's water-bearing capacity increases at high temperatures, causing humidity to rise. Plants thrive well in a relative humidity of up to 70%, but exceeding that affects their ability to transpire.

The ability to control air temperature and hence the humidity is the benefit only indoor hydroponics can provide.

Nutrient Management

Every aspect of hydroponics has its own importance, and none should be ranked lower than the other. All aspects collectively work together to yield wholesome growth. Still, if one is forced to choose one single aspect that contributes most toward the health of plants in hydroponics, that would be nutrients. Nutrients are a key success factor in hydroponics. An analogy can safely be drawn with our life carrier – our blood. Hydroponic nutrient composition is as important for plants as the composition of blood is for our own bodies.

Nutrients are the lifeblood of hydroponics.

Balanced nutrition for plants comprises a bouquet of individual elements that, when provided in the right amounts, are more than sufficient to replenish the soil.

MACRO nutrients are those that are absorbed in large quantities. These are:

Calcium (Ca): Essential for cell wall and membrane formation.

Magnesium (Mg): Essential for chlorophyll production by leaves. It also helps activate specific enzyme systems.

Nitrogen (N): Necessary for the formation of amino acids, coenzymes, and chlorophyll.

Phosphorus (P): For the production of sugar, phosphate, and ATP (energy). Enhances fruit production and root growth.

Potassium (K): For protein synthesis by plants, impacts plants' hardiness, root growth, and sugar manufacture.

MICRONUTRIENTS, also called trace elements, are consumed by plants in very small amounts. Plants absorb them in tiny quantities. Despite being consumed in small quantities, these are absolutely vital for performance. The right combination of micronutrients is the differentiator for successful hydroponics.

Boron (B): Necessary for the formation of cell walls when combined with calcium.

Copper (Cu): Copper activates the plant enzymes that are necessary for photosynthesis and respiration.

Iron (Fe): Chlorophyll formation, consumption of sugars through respiration to provide growth energy.

Manganese (Mn): It acts as a catalyst in the growth process of plants and the formation of oxygen in photosynthesis.

Molybdenum (Mo): It's the least consumed nutrient, but that's very good for nitrogen metabolism and fixation.

Sulfur (S): Sulfur is required for protein synthesis, water uptake, fruiting, and seeding, and acts as a natural fungicide.

Zinc (Zn): Chlorophyll formation, respiration, and nitrogen metabolism.

Carbon is absorbed by plants directly from the air and is utmost necessary for plant growth and respiration. Carbon, as part of CO_2, is the key ingredient of photosynthesis. Plants do not rely on hydroponic nutrients for carbon.

Given the importance of nutrients, it is often professed to keep a close eye on the composition of nutrients and to keep replenishing them on a real-time basis as and when they get consumed. That's where I again differ from these hydroponic gurus. Nutrient composition is indeed important, but there is really no need to get paranoid about regularly and online monitoring the composition of nutrients in a hydroponic solution and keep a keen eye for a close watch. Most hydroponic companies and enthusiasts lay emphasis on treating the hydroponic solution like a laboratory specimen – regularly measuring its TDS, checking its EC, checking the composition, using IOT devices that will automatically measure and transmit to your phone if nitrogen has reduced or if phosphorus is high, etc. Such regular online checking for precise control of composition also invites significant cost and involvement.

Is it really justified to be paranoid about nutrient monitoring?

Relax…

The answer lies in what we do to ourselves.

Do we monitor our blood composition on a daily basis?

One may argue that the analogy is incorrect because the body continuously regulates the blood composition – like through continuous synthesis of Red Blood Cells, White Blood Cells, Platelets in the bone marrow. Note, however, that our body does not regulate the 'nutrient' content in blood, like iron, ferritin, Potassium, Sodium, etc. It is replenished based on whatever comes in via oral intake. Whenever, in a couple of months, we take a blood test, we'll get a different composition of iron, ferritin, RBC, WBC, platelets, potassium, sodium, and so on. Some parameters are in range, and a few may border or even fall out of the range. That doesn't mean we had become dysfunctional in the meantime. The composition of blood is important but not a rigid number. Some people have low hemoglobin but function as well as other people with high hemoglobin.

The human body tolerates a range of nutrients.

The body doesn't immediately fail even if any nutrient goes out of range.

It is the body's metabolism that gets regulated in accordance with the nutrient availability.

The body regulates itself to survive and thrive on a range of nutrients.

That's the same with hydroponic nutrients.

Composition of hydroponic nutrients within a range is fine. Plants wouldn't wither away even if they are on reduced nutrient intake for a couple of hours, even days.

That's why I never advocate real-time monitoring of hydroponic nutrient composition. An occasional check is sufficient, say once every few days. Of course, the interval between the monitoring depends on other aspects – like what the plant density is in your system, what the reservoir volume in your system is, what stage of growth your plants are in, and the like. But the application of new-age technologies like IOT for monitoring the hydroponic solution is definitely something that I would never endorse – not even for large commercial farms.

People tend to follow the approach that if you are going big, you should adopt more innovations and more technologies. My view is rather to focus on the goal and to keep it simple. The goal is to grow plants using the hydroponic approach – with maximum profitability. Using technologies is not the goal. Everything costs money. Adding in sensors costs money. Maintaining those sensors costs money. Routine calibration of those sensors costs money. Nothing comes for free. The more technologies you add in, the more skilled manpower you would need to manage the system. The more gadgets you introduce in your hydroponic system, the more costly the system will become and the less possibility there would be of you making a profit.

How to Free Oneself from Nutrient Monitoring?

What can a hydroponic grower do to free themselves and not have to monitor the nutrients in the hydroponic solution frequently? That is very much possible. The grower can rest easy and let the hydroponic system take care of itself for days altogether without frequent intervention. For that, all that needs to be done is to maintain a high ratio of hydroponic solution versus plants. For every plant, keep as high a volume of hydroponic solution as possible. This simple approach is freedom from the hassle of continuously monitoring the health of the hydroponic solution. That's because when a large volume of hydroponic solution per plant is used, that builds in higher resilience within the system and the composition of the hydroponic solution will change much slower.

Of course, the frequency of monitoring depends on some other aspects – like what the plant density is in the hydroponic system, what the reservoir volume is in your system, what stage of growth the plants are in, and what the ambient temperature is. Plants consume water and nutrients while growing. The volume of the hydroponic solution available in the hydroponic system will reduce over time as the plants absorb water and nutrients. How the TDS varies depends on many factors and is very dynamic. TDS variation would be different in different stages of plant growth, varying depending on air temperature and also depending on the volume of the hydroponic solution used.

Consider a case when the ambient air temperature is hot, then the consumption of water is much more compared to the consumption of nutrients. So, as the volume of the hydroponic solution reduces, nutrients in the solution get concentrated in less water – meaning the strength of the solution may go up – meaning higher TDS. If there is a low volume of hydroponic solution per plant, the hydroponic solution gets depleted faster and the remaining hydroponic solution in your system becomes stronger and more hypertonic. That's not good. Roots can survive well on fewer nutrients, but if the solution contains high nutrients (hypertonic solution), there can be a possibility of reverse flow of nutrients – meaning nutrients can actually get leached out from roots. That's certainly not what plants want.

The situation would be opposite when the ambient air temperature is low. In this case, plants would consume significant amounts of nutrients, leading to a reduction of TDS in the solution over time.

Let's illustrate through a hypothetical example and, sorry, a little bit of maths becomes necessary.

Consider a hydroponic system that has 50 plants in a hydroponic solution of 100 liters of water + 100 grams of nutrients.

That's only 1 liter of hydroponic solution per plant, and TDS = 1000.

Say, every day, each plant drinks up 1 liter of water and 0.1 grams of nutrients – this is just representational and not actual.

At the end of the day, the hydroponic system will have 50 liters of water + 95 grams of nutrients, which comes to TDS = 1900.

TDS has increased from 1000 to 1900 during just one day, almost doubled. Such high TDS toward the latter part of the day would undoubtedly be detrimental for the roots of delicate plants like Lettuce, Spinach, Herbs, Pak Choi & the like.

As a result, to maintain the TDS relatively constant in this system, water will need to be topped up at least 2-3 times in a single day.

Now, let's see what happens if the volume of the hydroponic solution is tripled.

For this, consider 50 plants in a hydroponic solution of 300 liters of water + 300 grams of nutrients.

That's 3 liters of hydroponic solution per plant, and TDS = 1000 (same).

Every day, each plant drinks up the same amount, i.e., 1 liter of water and 0.1 grams of nutrients.

At the end of the day, the hydroponic system will have 250 liters of water + 295 grams of nutrients, which comes to TDS = 1180.

TDS has increased from 1000 to only 1180 during the day.

In this system, water will have to be topped up just once in 2-3 days because the system now has enough capacity and resilience to absorb the changes while reducing the variations in TDS.

To drive the point further, let's see what happens if the volume of the hydroponic solution is now increased to 5X.

For this, consider 50 plants in a hydroponic solution of 500 liters of water + 500 grams of nutrients.

That's 5 liters of hydroponic solution per plant, and TDS = 1000.

Every day, each plant drinks up the same amount, i.e., 1 liter of water and 0.1 grams of nutrients.

At the end of the day, the hydroponic system will have 450 liters of water + 495 grams of nutrients, which comes to TDS = 1100.

The increase in TDS has reduced. TDS has risen from 1000 to only 1100 during the day.

In this system, water will need to be topped up just once a week.

It's become evident through this exercise that all that needs to be done is to increase the size of the reservoir that holds the hydroponic solution – as big as possible. The same can be achieved by planting a smaller number of plants if there is a limitation in increasing the size of the reservoir that holds the hydroponic solution. This is a simple approach that builds inbuilt safety and resilience in the hydroponic solution – valid for hydroponic systems of all types. There would not be any need to install expensive online TDS meters or online nutrient analyzers by simply following this approach that prevents investment in expensive online meters, keeps the system straightforward, humanly predictable, and efficient.

An associated beneficial concept in this exercise should also be understood. When a high volume of hydroponic solution per plant is kept, there is also a considerable buffer of nutrients available in the system. This means there is no need to keep topping up nutrients because the system has a large stock of nutrients. The bigger the reservoir - comes closer to the 'Fill & Forget' zone as the volume of hydroponic solution per plant is increased. In the first example above where 100 liters of water + 100 grams of nutrients were used, there was a need to top-up nutrients every other day. But when the volume was increased by 5X, there would not be any need to top-up nutrients for more than a month! Plant roots also get to see a relatively constant TDS over a span of time, which is good for the plant as roots do not experience shocks.

Do NOT overdose nutrients. In hydroponics, 'more' is not better. A high concentration of nutrient solutions may exert reverse osmotic pressure on roots as it increases the TDS. Using low concentrations of nutrients (i.e., half-strength) is good for most plants. For example, in lettuce, gerbera, and geranium, nutrients may be reduced to 50% of the recommended values - without any adverse effects on biomass and quality.

There's another associated benefit that comes with this approach of keeping a high volume of hydroponic solution per plant. That's the constancy of pH. Variations in TDS induce associated variations in the pH of the solution. The pH of the hydroponic solution needs to be kept in the range of 4 to 6.5 to prevent nutrient precipitation. When there is a LOW volume of hydroponic solution per plant, there will be a tendency for either the anions or the cations to build up when the volume of hydroponic solution reduces. That's because depending on the growth stage of the plant, it will pick up either more anions or more cations. Having a high volume of hydroponic solution per plant addresses this issue to a large extent.

How frequently one needs to monitor the hydroponic solution will change drastically depending on whether the user is engaged in indoor hydroponics or outdoor hydroponics. It should be easy to grasp this now. In indoor hydroponics, the ambient air temperature is either controlled as in polyhouses, or it's not as high as in outdoor hydroponics even if the temperature is not controlled. Plants transpire less and lose less water in indoor hydroponics, resulting in lower changes in the composition of the hydroponic solution compared to outdoor hydroponics. For that reason, monitoring the nutrient health becomes less onerous and less frequent in indoor hydroponics.

What has been learned so far in this discussion is important. We have learned that it is possible to do hydroponics without much difficulty if we choose a large reservoir to hold the hydroponic solution. The larger, the better. This simple solution provides the freedom from having to monitor TDS too frequently and will also ensure that the hydroponic solution remains rich in nutrients – without becoming too rich – irrespective of the day being hot or cold.

This is the key takeaway from this discussion: an important takeaway.

It is indeed a difficult exercise to keep track of the variations in TDS & water volume with resulting pH changes and to be able to predict when to top-up nutrients. Actually, the above-mentioned 3 exercises were deliberately made simple to allow anyone to easily grasp the subject and its importance. This was made simple by not considering the hardness of water. Water has its own hardness, and water hardness is not useful for the plants. Every time water is topped up into the hydroponic solution, that introduces more & more hardness that comes along with the water that is used to top-up. How does one keep track of variations of the TDS due to nutrients and the build-up of TDS due to the hardness of water? This is actually the most difficult part of nutrient management – unfortunately never talked about in any online or offline professional hydroponic discourse – because who knows the solution!

Analysis of TDS due to nutrients and the build-up of TDS due to the hardness of water over a period of time gets impacted also by ambient conditions. If the ambient temperature is hot, plants lose more water through transpiration from their leaves – to keep themselves cool in a hot environment. If the ambient temperature is cool, plants lose less water through transpiration. In both situations, the plant would consume nearly the same amount of nutrients – because nutrient uptake is related to plant metabolic requirements and not linked to water loss by transpiration. The transpiration rate thus gets added to the already difficult situation that we were attempting to address. Understanding all the aspects involved in hydroponics is, after all, the key objective of this book. Understanding the difficulties leads one to look for the path, the solution. Most companies that sell hydroponic guidance seldom cover such key aspects. As a result, hydroponics remains a subject of hit and trial for the majority of enthusiasts, eventually leading to abandonment.

Having understood the complexities introduced in TDS management due to water hardness and ambient temperature, how does one handle that? Companies selling nutrients just talk about the dosing rates of nutrients, without telling how to measure the TDS due to nutrients versus TDS due to water hardness. That's important to know, but very difficult to calculate by any hydroponics.

That's where GreenLoop Hydroponic Nutrients are a differentiator.

GreenLoop has developed a unique and very easy method to calculate how much of useful nutrients versus how much useless hardness (from water) remains in your hydroponic solution at any point in time. For this purpose, GreenLoop provides its proprietary Nutrient Management Calculator to all its users, for free. This calculator is a simple Excel sheet in which the user has to enter just 2 values – TDS and the volume of water topped up to bring the level back to the top of the hydroponic system/tank. Every time the user observes that the level of the hydroponic solution in the tank has gone down, just measure the TDS and then measure the volume of water that has been topped up to bring the level back to the top of the hydroponic system/tank.

Feed the TDS and volume of water into the calculator, and it will tell exactly how much useful nutrients remain in your hydroponic solution and how much nutrients should be added. After a few weeks, there would reach a time when the nutrients would need to be replaced due to excessive hardness build-up – and the calculator will tell that too. It really can't get simpler.

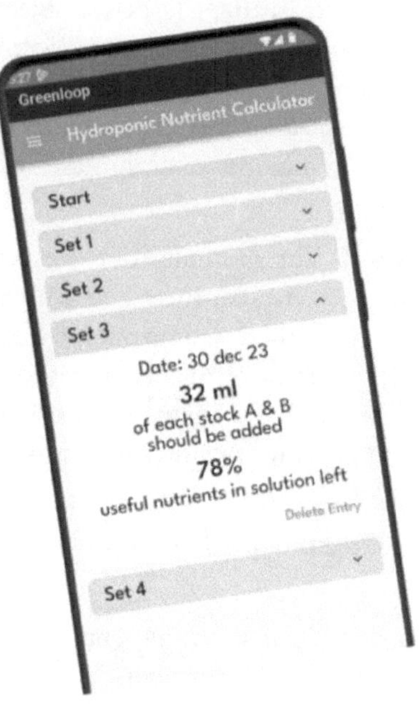

When using this calculator, the user does not have to bother about complicated aspects like EC, nutrient consumption by plants, TDS accumulation, useful versus useless TDS, how much water loss through transpiration, different readings by different TDS meters, etc. The GreenLoop Nutrient Calculator considers all this, so the user is free. The entire history of top-ups becomes available to users to see within the calculator, for reference. This calculator is very useful for hobbyists as well as professional hydroponics and allows the user to accurately know the condition of the nutrient solution – resulting in a stable and assured hydroponic experience.

The only precaution that needs to be exercised when using this calculator is to use the same TDS meter every time. That's because different TDS meters of different brands show different readings.

This calculator from GreenLoop is available in the form of an Excel file and also as a phone app. This simple app works on a mobile phone – and it does the same job as the Excel file – it tells exactly how much of useful nutrients versus how much useless hardness remains in the hydroponic solution at any point in time, how many nutrients to add, and when to replace them.

The calculator and the app were introduced at the end because the objective was for the user to first understand all the basics and intricacies involved. The background workings of the calculator file and app are proprietary; hence, this description sufficiently informs the user about all that is being done in the background of this calculator/app.

If this simple calculator/app had been revealed initially, the user might have chosen to skip the entire discussion and proceeded to use the calculator file/app. But that would not have served the purpose of becoming knowledgeable in the subject.

There's one more aspect of nutrient management that one should be conscious of. Commercial nutrients come in generally two-part or three-part solutions, and several nutrient manufacturers specify that the nutrient solution composition should be changed at different stages of plant growth or for different types of plants. For that purpose, nutrient manufacturers provide different sets of nutrients for different stages or specify different quantities of the parts of the solution to be used. Manufacturers obviously make more money by selling different products to do the same job. Should one really need to switch to different grades of nutrients during different stages of plant growth or for different plants? The answer is that you need to follow the manufacturer's recommendations because the manufacturers have composed their nutrients that way. GreenLoop again offers the easiest approach, as GreenLoop Hydroponic Nutrients do not require the user to change the nutrient composition at any stage of plant growth and are equally suitable for all plant types. Just think of it, would anyone change the soil to a different type of soil for different stages of growing plants? It doesn't need an answer; it's obvious. Using the same approach, GreenLoop has developed the proprietary combination that works for all plants, all stages of growth with the same strength.

All nutrient suppliers provide the method of using their nutrients, and users should refer to that. These instructions are based on manufacturers' years of experience in the field. For the sake of completeness, presented herewith is how to use the GreenLoop Hydroponic Nutrients that are most popular with users in India.

Usage of GreenLoop Hydroponic Nutrients

There are 2 types of GreenLoop Hydroponic Nutrients.

Both types can be used interchangeably for all kinds of plants.

- GreenLoop Hydroponic Nutrients **Leafy-200**: Better for leafy plants.

- GreenLoop Leafy-200 Nutrients **Tomato & Veggies**: Better for Tomatoes.

Usage for both types is the same.

These nutrients come as solid mixtures in 2 separate bottles, i.e., two-part nutrients.

Solid mixtures mean that when a user gets them, they have the maximum activity compared to liquid solutions.

The first step is to prepare the stock solutions (concentrate) that remain okay for a year or more, as long as they are kept in the shade. A small dosage of these stock solutions is used to make the 'Hydroponic Solution'.

Dissolve each solid bottle separately in one liter of water each – that makes 2 separate bottles of concentrate – one yellow and the other dark red. It is better to use RO water or boiled (& cooled) water for the maximum longevity of these concentrates.

Now, to make a HALF-strength hydroponic solution - which suits all plants for all growth stages - mix 5 ml of each concentrate per liter of water taken.

For example, if the intention is to make a 50-liter half-strength hydroponic solution:

Add Stock A = 5 ml x 50 = 250 ml

Add Stock B = 5 ml x 50 = 250 ml

Another example: If the intention is to make a 20-liter half-strength hydroponic solution:

Add Stock A = 5 ml × 20 = 100 ml

Add Stock B = 5 ml × 20 = 100 ml

Though a half-strength solution is sufficient, some users want to increase the strength for certain plants like tomatoes that thrive in both low and high TDS. The addition of concentrate can be increased accordingly.

For example, if the intention is to make a 50-liter full-strength hydroponic solution:

Add Stock A = 10 ml x 50 = 500 ml

Add Stock B = 10 ml × 50 = 500 ml

Thereafter, just use the GreenLoop Nutrient Management Calculator to manage the hydroponic solution.

For convenience, GreenLoop provides 2 methods of nutrient management:

1.   SIMPLE METHOD – without TDS meter.

2.   ACCURATE METHOD.

SIMPLE METHOD – without a TDS meter:

- Prepare a HALF-strength hydroponic solution. Use soft water with TDS < 100 (or 200 max).

  Prepare 2-3 liters of hydroponic solution per plant. For example, if you have 10 plants, your system should hold 20-30 liters of hydroponic solution. For big plants like tomatoes, use more. For vines like cucumbers, use at least 5 liters of hydroponic solution per plant. More is better.

- For the first 2-3 weeks, top-up occasionally with <u>water</u> only to bring back the water level in the tank.

- Then, every week, add 1 ml of each stock solution per liter of the hydroponic solution.

  For big plants like tomatoes, brinjal, and vines, put 2ml of each stock per liter per week. Keep topping up with water regularly.

- Replace the hydroponic solution entirely after about 10-12 weeks, then start over again following the previous steps.

Example

- *For 10 plants, make a HALF-strength hydroponic solution of 25 liters.*

- *For the first 2-3 weeks, top-up plain soft water to bring back the level in the tank, say every 2-3 days.*

- *Third week onwards, add 1-2 ml of each stock solution <u>per week</u>, per liter of hydroponic solution. That's 25 ml of each stock in this example. Top-up with soft water every 2-3 days.*

- *After 10-12 weeks, replace the solution fully and start over again.*

Typical Dosing Schedule.

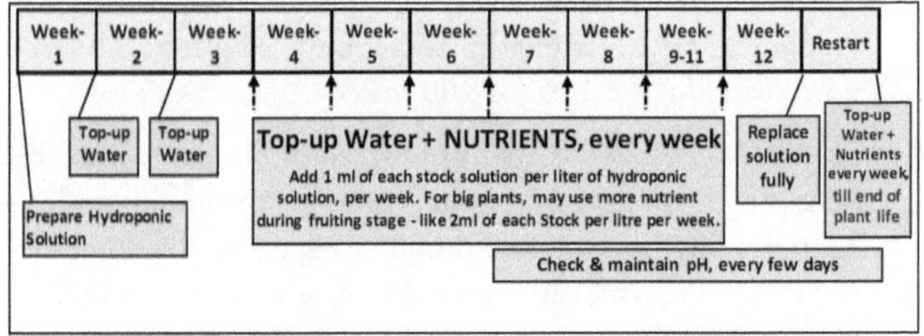

Accurate Method

Follow the simple method as above + <u>USE A TDS METER (4-digit)</u>.

And use the GreenLoop Nutrient Calculator app or Excel file.

This method allows the user to use the hydroponic solution over a longer time, more cost-effectively.

GreenLoop Calculator tells you how many nutrients to dose, how many 'useful' nutrients remain in the solution, and when to replace it entirely.

Growing in Media Bed (Coco Peat etc):

Use half-strength solution to water the bed – just once every 7-10 days initially and increase the frequency when plants are big. Use plain water to water the bed on other days whenever the bed appears dry. Keep the bottom drain hole open to prevent waterlogging. Once every 3-4 weeks, wet the bed thoroughly with normal water (this refreshes the bed by washing out leftover unused nutrients and prevents build-up) and then after 2-3 hours, add the half-strength nutrients again to the bed.

Additional useful information:

> Using soft water gives the best results, allowing the use of nutrients for a longer time. Municipal water is generally soft. Groundwater may be hard.
>
> **<u>If you do not have soft water</u>**, please replace the hydroponic solution slightly earlier - as per the following guide:
>
> a) If the water TDS is 100-200, replace the nutrient solution after 10 weeks.
>
> b) If the water TDS is between 200 and 400, replace the nutrient solution after 8 weeks.
>
> c) If the water TDS is 400 or more, it is better to use a TDS meter.

Now that we understand principally all details regarding the hydroponic elements, let's tabulate here below the ideal ranges of these parameters for various plant types. These tables are the generally recommended EC, TDS, pH for various plants that I had collated and experimented with during the early days of my hydroponic journey. Actually, these are the kind of freely available hydroponic guidance that succeed in getting a budding hydroponic flummoxed. These tables are not really necessary when using GreenLoop Hydroponic Nutrients, as they work well for all plant types. But referring to these tables would help the commercial hydroponic in extending the life of the nutrient solution, thereby increasing profits. Like in the case of tomatoes, because very high TDS can be tolerated by plants, there is latitude available to accommodate more water hardness build-up in the same nutrient solution for a longer time – where GreenLoop's unique nutrient management Pant App becomes really useful. If in doubt, refer to the nutrient management section once again for the concept.

———◆◆———

Recommended TDS, EC, pH - Leafy and Veggies
(For Low to Medium TDS range)

Plants	pH	EC, mS/cm	Minimum PPM	Maximum PPM
Lettuce	5.5-6.5	0.8-1.2	560	840
Artichoke	6.5-7.5	0.8-1.8	560	1260
Radish	6.0-7.0	1.6-2.2	840	1540
Sweet Corn	6.0	1.6-2.4	840	1680
Pea	6.0-7.0	0.8-1.8	980	1260
Asparagus	6.0-6.8	1.4-1.8	980	1260
Garlic	6.0	1.4-1.8	980	1260
Leek	6.5-7.0	1.4-1.8	980	1260
Onions	6.0-6.7	1.4-1.8	980	1260
Parsnip	6.0	1.4-1.8	980	1260
Cauliflower	6.0-7.0	0.5-2.0	1050	1400
Pak-choi	7.0	1.5-2.0	1050	1400
Pak Choi	7	1.5-2.0	1050	1400
Carrots	6.3	1.6-2.0	1120	1400
Carrot	6.3	1.6-2.0	1120	1400
Cucumber	5.8-6.0	1.7-2.5	1190	1750
Beetroot	6.0-6.5	0.8-5	1260	3500
Celery	6.5	1.8-2.4	1260	1680
Fodder	6.0	1.8-2.0	1260	1400
Broad Bean	6.0-6.5	1.8-2.2	1260	1540
Capsicum	6.0-6.5	1.8-2.2	1260	1540

Recommended TDS, EC, pH - Leafy and Veggies
(For Medium to High TDS range)

Plants	pH	EC, mS/cm	Min PPM	Max PPM
Spinach	5.5-6.6	1.8-2.3	1260	1610
Silverbeet	6.0-7.0	1.8-2.3	1260	1610
Marrow	6.0	1.8-2.4	1260	1680
Pumpkin	5.5-7.5	1.8-2.4	1260	1680
Turnip	6.0-6.5	1.8-2.4	1260	1680
Zucchini	6.0	1.8-2.4	1260	1680
Bean	6	2.0-4.0	1260	2800
Endive	5.5	2.0-2.4	1400	1680
Okra	6.5	2.0-2.4	1400	1680
Bell peppers	6.0-6.5	2.0-2.5	1400	1750
Potato	5.0-6.0	2.0-2.5	1400	1750
Sweet Potato	5.5-6.0	2.0-2.5	1400	1750
Peppers	5.8-6.3	2.0-3.0	1400	2100
Pepino	6.0-6.5	2.0-5.0	1400	3500
Tomato	5.5-6.5	2.0-5.0	1400	3500
Bean (Common)	6.0	2-4	1400	2800
Beans (Italian bush)	6.0-6.5	2-4	1400	2800
Beans (Lima)	6.0-6.5	2-4	1400	2800
Beans (Pole)	6.0-6.5	2-4	1400	2800
Brussell Sprout	6.5-7.5	2.5-3.0	1750	2100
Cabbage	6.5-7.0	2.5-3.0	1750	2100
Taro	5.0-5.5	2.5-3.0	1750	2100
Brussel Sprout	6.5	2.5-3.0	1750	2100
Eggplant	5.5-6.5	2.5-3.5	1750	2450
Broccoli	6.0-6.5	2.8-3.5	1960	2450
Hot Peppers	6.0-6.5	3.0-3.5	2100	2450

Recommended TDS, EC, pH - Herbs

Plants	pH	EC, mS/cm	Min PPM	Max PPM
Watercress	6.5-6.8	0.4-1.8	280	1260
Thyme	5.5-7.0	0.8-1.6	560	1120
Parsley	5.5-6.0	0.8-1.8	560	1260
Sage	5.5-6.5	1.0-1.4	700	1120
Fennel	6.4-6.8	1.0-1.4	700	980
Lavender	6.4-6.8	1.0-1.4	700	980
Basil	5.5-6.5	1.0-1.6	700	1120
Lemon Balm	5.5-6.5	1.0-1.6	700	1120
Rosemary	5.5-6.0	1.0-1.6	700	1120
Mustard Cress	6.0-6.5	1.2-2.4	840	1680
Marjoram	6.0	1.6-2.0	1120	1400
Chives	6.0-6.5	1.8-2.4	1260	1540
Mint	5.5-6.0	2.0-2.4	1400	1680
Chicory	5.5-60	2.0-2.4	1400	1600

Recommended TDS, EC, pH - Fruiting Plants

Plants	pH	EC, mS/cm	Min PPM	Max PPM
Rhubarb	5.0- 6.0	1.6-2.0	840	1400
Black Currant	6	1.4-1.8	980	1260
Red Currant	6	1.4-1.8	980	1260
Watermelon	5.8	1.5-2.4	1260	1680
Blueberry	4.0 -5.0	1.8-2.0	1260	1400
Strawberries	5.5-6.5	1.8-2.2	1260	1540
Melon	5.5-6.0	2.0-2.5	1400	1750

Recommended TDS, EC, pH - Flowering Plants

Plants	pH	EC, mS/cm	Min PPM	Max PPM
Cymbidiums	5.5	0.6-1.0	420	560
Bromeliads	5.0-7.5	0.8-1.2	560	840
Freesia	6.5	1.0-2.0	700	1400
African Violets	6.0-7.0	1.2-1.5	840	1050
Begonia	6.5	1.4-2.4	980	1260
Dahlia	6.0-7.0	1.5-2.0	1050	1400
Roses	5.5-6.0	1.5-2.5	1050	1750
Anthurium	5.0-6.0	1.6-2.0	1120	1400
Antirrhinum	6.5	1.6-2.0	1120	1400
Caladium	6.0-7.5	1.6-2.0	1120	1400
Ferns	6.0	1.6-2.0	1120	1400
Palms	6.0-7.5	1.6-2.0	1120	1400
Stock	6.0-7.0	1.6-2.0	1120	1400
Ficus	5.5-6.0	1.6-2.4	1120	1680
Impatiens	5.5-6.5	1.8-2.0	1260	1400
Aphelandra	5.0-6.0	1.8-2.4	1260	1680
Aster	6.0-6.5	1.8-2.4	1260	1680
Canna	6.0	1.8-2.4	1260	1680
Carnation	6.0	2.0-3.5	1260	2450
Dieffenbachia	5.0	1.8-2.0	1400	1680
Dracaena	5.0-6.0	1.8-2.4	1400	1680
Monstera	5.0-6.0	1.8-2.4	1400	1680
Chrysanthemum	6.0-6.2	1.8-2.5	1400	1750
Gladiolus	5.5-6.5	2.0-2.4	1400	1680
Gerbera	5.0-6.5	2.0-2.5	1400	1750

Nutrient Deficiency Symptoms

Following the nutrient management regimen as illustrated thus far should keep a person free from having to worry about the deficiency symptoms in plants. For the sake of completeness of information, it would be good to include here the typical symptoms that come about due to deficiency of the various nutrients.

Nitrogen:

Deficiency: General chlorosis of lower leaves. Plants are slow-growing, weak, and stunted. Yellowing of leaves occurs, particularly affecting the older leaves first. Yield is low, and plants reach maturity early.

Excess (Toxicity): Too much nitrogen may burn the leaves. The stem becomes weak, but plants may appear darker green. New leaves would appear soft and succulent. Fruit and seed crops may not produce.

Phosphorous:

Deficiency: symptoms are usually more noticeable in young plants. Plants become slow-growing (both leaves and stems) and appear stunted. Older leaves are affected first and may turn purplish in discoloration. Leaves tend to become curled and small-sized.

Excess (Toxicity): Excess Phosphorus will lead to reduced absorption of Iron, Manganese, and Zinc, resulting in their deficiency.

Potassium:

Deficiency: Initially, there are generally no visible symptoms of potassium deficiency, despite there being a deficiency. The plant would just appear to have a slow growth rate. Chlorosis and necrosis show up in later stages of plant development. Chlorotic symptoms typically begin on the leaf tip. Then, older leaf margins appear to be burned out with localized chlorotic or mottled areas.

Excess (Toxicity): Excess potassium will lead to reduced absorption of magnesium and calcium, resulting in their deficiency.

Calcium:

Deficiency: Starts showing in young leaves that become irregularly shaped and may become quite dark green. Tips of the young leaves will get dry and brittle. Even the roots start dying. The stem of the plant becomes weak.

Excess (Toxicity): Results in magnesium and/or potassium deficiency symptoms.

Magnesium:

Deficiency: Symptoms appear as interveinal chlorosis. Older leaf margins become yellow or reddish-purple between the veins; this means the midrib will remain green. Some leaves may curl and have reddish undersides, while others may show twisted veins with brittleness in the leaves.

Excess (Toxicity): None.

Molybdenum:

Deficiency: Molybdenum deficiency symptoms are similar to Nitrogen deficiency. Specifically, leaves may become pale and brittle, eventually withering from the sides, leaving only the central vein of the leaves.

Excess (Toxicity): Generally, no symptoms in moderate toxicity. In extreme toxicity conditions, plants may show stunted growth with discoloration.

Sulfur:

Deficiency: Symptoms are extremely difficult to detect as they resemble the symptoms of Nitrogen and Molybdenum deficiencies. They appear in younger leaves that turn light green to yellow with stems becoming woody. Sulfur deficiency can cause plants to become small with thin stems.

Excess (Toxicity): Premature leaf death.

Iron:

Deficiency: Leaves exhibit yellowing between the veins – called interveinal chlorosis. This happens as chlorophyll production gets reduced due to iron deficiency. Particularly in young leaves, there appears a sharp color difference between the veins of the leaf and chlorotic areas.

Excess (Toxicity): None.

Manganese:

Deficiency: Interveinal chlorosis in young leaves is a common symptom, but with almost no color difference between veins and interveinal areas.

Excess (Toxicity): Blackish-brown spots with yellow rings around them, or sometimes red spots, will appear on the older leaves. Chlorosis and necrotic lesions may also appear on the leaves.

Boron:

Deficiency: Boron deficiency typically leads to the death of the terminal bud – which is the main growing part of the plant. Leaves may become dark brown with irregular lesions. Stems may grow brittle, and the plant would exhibit stunted growth. The base of the leaves may show whitish-yellow spots. Sometimes, flower buds fail to form or become irregularly shaped.

Excess (Toxicity): Excess of Boron will lead to chlorosis in leaves followed by necrosis. Boron toxicity results in chlorosis followed by necrosis. Symptoms start showing from the leaf tip and leaf margins. Gradually, the symptoms expand toward the central vein of the leaves, making them appear scorched. Ultimately, the leaves start falling off prematurely.

Zinc:

Deficiency: Hormone production in plants gets affected, leading to interveinal chlorosis. Young leaves exhibit yellowing between the veins, which starts showing from the middle of leaves. Plant growth is impacted and appears stunted. Severe zinc deficiency will cause the leaves to become grayish white in color; eventually, the leaves will fall prematurely.

Excess (Toxicity): Moderate toxicity of Zinc does not generally show any symptoms. Excess (Toxicity) of copper will lead to Iron deficiency. High toxicity can lead to leaves showing chlorosis, interveinal chlorosis, and reduced growth of roots.

Copper:

Deficiency: The plant exhibits melanosis (brown discoloration) in some cases. Chlorosis appears in the young leaves, with plant growth becoming slow. Leaves can get distorted, and young shoots appear to die off.

Excess (Toxicity): Excess (Toxicity) of copper will lead to a deficiency of other metals in the plants, particularly leading to iron deficiency. As a result, iron deficiency symptoms start showing.

Nutrient Recipe by Self

If the user wishes to prepare the nutrients themselves, the following recipe may be used for preparing the hydroponic solution. This recipe would generally suit all kinds of plants. This recipe is not the same as GreenLoop Nutrients.

Water = 100 Liters

Calcium Nitrate = 90 g

Magnesium Sulfate = 55 g

Monoammonium Phosphate = 10 g

Mono Potassium Phosphate = 15 g

Potassium Nitrate = 15 g

Potassium Sulfate = 65 g

Chelated Micronutrient mixture = 300 g

Fe 12% = 4 g

To make this recipe by oneself, the user will need to find the right ingredients. These are available in a variety of purities, such as laboratory grade, Analytical grade, Reagent grade, Industrial grade, etc. Users must look at the composition of the ingredient they are buying and adjust it according to the purity available. If an ingredient is... let's say 97% pure, then 97% is what the user is putting in the solution, and the remaining 3% is unknown. Hydroponics is done to get the best purity of veggies, so it would make sense to buy ingredients with the highest possible purity – but they are expensive, especially in small packaging. Therefore, most commonly, people resort to buying the ordinary commercial ingredients that are usually used as farm fertilizers to be mixed with soil – and there the purpose gets lost. Nutrient manufacturing companies have the benefit of buying high-quality ingredients in bulk and getting the bulk benefit for cost reduction, which a small buyer does not get.

Evident from the tabulation above is that the user needs a few grams of each ingredient to make the hydroponic solution, while the minimum packaging that comes is usually in kilograms. What does the user do with the balance of the package? How long can it be kept usefully? Activity would go down with the passage of time, surely. The user will end up keeping containers of various ingredients in the store, to be taken out, weighed in grams, and then to be packed back again. Weighing tiny grams is by itself a challenge. If the fan is running overhead, the changing air pressure by itself will change the reading of the micro weighing machine that the user would be using.

Sight and feel of the same ingredient would appear different from different companies. For example, Magnesium Sulfate comes as yellow powder as well as white powder. One would wonder which is right and matches the composition at hand.

While mixing the ingredients, there is a risk of nutrient lock-out. This means that a high concentration of any one type of nutrient in water may sometimes preferentially react with the next ingredient that the user is putting in water. For example, Calcium nitrate will have the propensity to start locking with sulfates and phosphates. So, it is better to add all of them separately in water and then combine them to minimize the risk. People do wonder sometimes why the plants are not growing well despite having added all ingredients to the water to make the solution – and now you know the possible reason. Here again, nutrient manufacturing companies have the edge because they have formulated the nutrients and provided a solution that is easily implementable without risk.

Actually, nutrients are a small cost out of the total cost of doing hydroponics. The estimate is that nutrients account for hardly 10% of the total cost involved. So why risk the remaining 90% by making the nutrients yourselves? The recommendation would be to opt for commercially available, established, and proven hydroponic nutrients, and just get on with it rather than spending time and effort making the nutrients yourself and inviting risk. Most commercial companies provide their hydroponic nutrients in bulk supply at half the retail cost, making it easy.

Grow Lights

Photosynthesis is a crucial process for all life on Earth to exist. It allows plants to harness energy from sunlight and convert it into biochemical energy, which supports nearly every living organism. Plants consume carbon dioxide from the air, water from the medium, and release oxygen into the atmosphere while manufacturing glucose (a sugar) that is used for plant growth and storage within the plants. That's the basic photosynthesis. Chlorophyll, found in chloroplasts within plant cells, absorbs energy from sunlight. During photosynthesis, chlorophyll captures energy from blue and red light waves. Green light is mostly reflected back, and that is what gives plants their characteristic green color. Chlorophyll converts light energy into chemical energy (ATP and NADPH) that assembles glucose using carbon dioxide, through reactions that take place in the stroma that is located within the chloroplast of plant cells.

Succinctly put, light energy drives photosynthesis.

Insufficient light can lead to growth retardation or death in plants. Different plants have varying light requirements (photoperiod and intensity) for optimal growth. White light is the combination of all colors of light. When unsure, use white lights for hydroponics, though that wouldn't be optimum for growth. Sunlight contains all the wavelengths required by plants, and hence remains the best choice to grow plants. Where sunlight is deficient or its intensity is not beneficial to plants due to the prevailing environment, the grower has to resort to using artificial lights, also called grow lights. Grow lights come in various types, intensities, and wavelengths. For proper hydroponics, using the appropriate grow light pertinent to the plants being cultivated becomes crucial.

The primary benefit of using indoor grow lights is that it gives the grower complete control over the horticultural growing environment. The use of these, coupled with the right air temperature conditions inside the polyhouse, will simulate the natural growing seasons, allowing a year-round supply of fresh veggies, herbs, and flowers. Grow lights allow the grower to enhance the growing conditions. Instead of 8-hour natural sunlight, grow lights allow the grower to provide double the duration of light to plants or more, which reduces the growing time. Most plants grow best when exposed to 16-18 hrs of light per day. Increasing growing hours further than that does not translate much into plant growth. For flowering plants, the duration of daylight should not be kept more than 12-14 hours, as flowering plants exhibit photoperiodism – that is, they need periods of total darkness cycle for the correct formation of flowers and fruits.

In earlier days, metal halide type and high-intensity discharge type of grow lights were used, which are prohibitively expensive and generate lots of heat. Metal Halide (MH) lamps emit primarily blue light, which is suitable for the vegetative growth stage. High-Pressure Sodium (HPS) lamps emit primarily red light – that's suitable for flowering and fruiting during the plant reproductive stage. After the advent of LEDs, the usage of metal halide grow lights and High-Pressure Sodium (HPS) lamps has reduced to a trickle, so there is no need to describe them further here.

LED grow lights come in all kinds of wavelengths, available as per requirement. LED grow lights are not very expensive when compared to their earlier metal halide counterparts. LED grow lights are also energy-efficient and do not generate much heat, thus helping the cause of hydroponics.

For practical purposes of hydroponics, the light spectrum ranges from wavelengths of 380 nm to 780 nm. The UV range starts even deeper at 180 nm, while the infrared range goes beyond 780 nm.

Red has a wavelength of 600-680 nm.

Blue light has a wavelength of 380-480 nm.

Higher wavelength ranges, such as 600-680 nm, are good for the flowering and fruiting stages of plants.

The lower-wavelength range, such as 380-480 nm, is good for leafy plants and for the vegetative growth of plants.

Most growers use lower-wavelength lights during the stage when the plant is growing and then introduce higher wavelengths of light when plants start flowering. A point to note here is that lower wavelengths of light would always be required because the leaves continue to grow even after flowering and would always require lower wavelengths. During the flowering stage, about half of the low-wavelength lights are generally replaced by higher wavelength lights by commercial growers. With further advancements in LED technology, now LED tubes are available that change their wavelengths with just a flick of a button – within the same LED tube. That's really convenient and should be the default choice of LED tubes to be considered for hydroponics, while also reducing the inventory cost for growers.

Above is the crux of all light-related aspects.

Once you choose LED tubes with switchable wavelengths, that's it for all the flexibility a person needs for hydroponics. Readers might have heard of blue lights, red lights, green lights, far-red lights, and about tubes that are a mix of all these. These are just a combination play of various kinds of wavelengths. The intention here is to simplify hydroponics for the reader, so there should be no point in delving deeper into aspects like blue lights triggering hormone growth and inhibiting dormancy, or red lights aiding pigment formation and flower development, etc. During the summer months, blue light is most prominent when the sun is at its highest point in the sky and suits vegetative growth of plants. Red light, which occurs when the sun is lower in the sky, plays a crucial role in triggering plant reproduction, leading to the formation of flowers and fruits.

Talking about light intensity, provide as much high-intensity as possible. Light intensity is the power (watt) supplied per square foot of the planting area and is measured in power (watts) per square foot. Providing 20 watts per square foot is sufficient for most plants. Providing up to 40 watts per square foot may be practiced, depending on one's budget and the cost of electricity that can be tolerated. The higher the intensity, the better the growth of plants. For example, a row of plants having one LED tube above them would grow slower compared to a similar row of plants having double LED tubes above them.

Light should be focused on the plants, rather than frittering away in the vicinity. Reflectors help in this by focusing the light on the plant and should be integrated with the LED tubes. It serves well to paint the area around using white paint to increase the reflectivity of surroundings. White reflects 70-80% of light falling on it. Yellow reflects 65-70%. Aluminum foil reflects around 60-65%. Black would absorb all the light and reflect hardly 10%.

Installation of grow lights allows the grower to grow plants that are totally out of season. Be it rainy months or periods of low sunshine, grow lights allow the plant production to go on uninterrupted.

Material

The target of hydroponics is to get contamination-free veggies, making it necessary that appropriate materials are deployed for the purpose. The main concern is the chemicals that might leach out from the plastic used, particularly the lead that is common during the manufacturing process of PVC.

Equipment suppliers use the term 'Food-grade plastic' quite liberally. Every country has regulations for this, and in India, there are the 'Food Safety and Standards (Packaging) Regulations' which specify the method of testing as per IS 9845. This standard specifies the methods to determine the migration of plastic constituents when they come in contact with foodstuffs. A suggestive list of plastic constituents whose migration needs to be limited is provided in the 'Food Safety and Standards (Packaging) Regulations'. These constituents include Barium, Cobalt, Copper, Iron, Lithium, Manganese, Zinc, Antimony, Phthalic acid, bis (2-ethylhexyl) ester (DEHP) - and their limits are prescribed therein. According to the 'Food Safety and Standards (Packaging) Regulations', products made of recycled plastics shall not be used for articles of food.

'Food Safety and Standards (Packaging) Regulations' are quite comprehensive, covering a variety of construction materials and should be referred to by a professional grower intending to set-up the commercial hydroponic set-up.

In hydroponics, it's the hydroponic solution that contacts the plastic or other material of which the hydroponic system is made up. In this context, the following extract from the 'Food Safety and Standards (Packaging) Regulations' appears most relevant:

Provided that Drinking Water (both Packaged and Mineral Water) shall be packed in colorless, transparent, and tamper-proof bottles or containers made of polyethylene (PE) conforming to IS: 10146, polyvinyl chloride (PVC) conforming to IS: 10151, polyalkylene terephthalate (PET and PBT) conforming to IS: 12252, polypropylene (PP) conforming to IS: 10910, food-grade polycarbonate conforming to IS: 14971, polystyrene conforming to IS: 10142, or sterile glass bottles only. The transparency of a container shall not be less than 85 percent in light transmittance:

Depending on the material, PVC, PE, Polycarbonate, PET, PBT, or polystyrene, the user may refer to the appropriate standards relevant to these materials.

PVC pipes and channels are commonly used in hydroponics, and most relevant for this is the Indian Standard IS 4985 (UNPLASTICIZED PVC PIPES FOR POTABLE WATER SUPPLIES). When going to the market to buy the PVC pipes to construct the hydroponic system, you should ask for only the IS 4985 pipes, as these are meant for drinking water and contain the least permissible amount of lead plasticizer. While there is no Indian Standard for PVC Channels for drinking water, it's best to ensure that the PVC channels under consideration contain impurities in conformance with the IS 4985 standard.

There are some studies that suggest that the leaching of chemicals from plastic into water happens at high temperatures, like 70 degrees Celsius, and is barely observable at low temperatures as encountered in hydroponics. Still, when opting for it, it is better to choose standard certified materials.

Caution: Never ever think of making the hydroponic systems using cement or concrete – as these materials spoil the hydroponic solution by raising its pH.

———◆◆———

Growing from seeds

Believe it or not, growing saplings from seeds remains the most difficult part of hydroponics. Another way to look at it is that if you can grow plants from seeds, you can well do the hydroponics easily. One may argue that it's not so. Everyone has different experiences. This is the experience shared by many people, so it gives some credence to it.

Seeds have an expiry that tends to get overlooked. Old seeds may not germinate as well as the new ones. For this reason, it's advisable to buy a new cache of seeds every season rather than using the old leftovers from the previous season. Seeds grow best in a neutral pH environment – something that cocopeat provides very well. Cocopeat is pH neutral and the best medium to grow seeds on. A common mistake people make while growing seeds is to push them too deep into cocopeat. Don't push them too deep. A good rule of thumb is to keep the depth of seeds equal to the size of the seeds. The bigger the seeds, the deeper they should be planted inside cocopeat. The smaller the seed, the shallower their depth should be. Ensure to keep the medium moist and warm at all times. Most seeds grow well between 10-30 degrees Celsius temperature.

You may refer to the following charts to find the recommended growing conditions for various types of seeds.

	Germination Temperature, °C [23]			Days to germinate under optimum temperature and moisture conditions [24]
	Minimum	Optimum	Maximum	
Bean, Lima	16	29	29	6
Bean, Snap	16	27	35	7
Beets	4	29	35	4
Broccoli		29		4
Brussels Sprouts		27		4
Cabbage	4	27	38	4
Carrot	4	27	35	6
Cauliflower	4	27	38	5
Celeriac		21		11
Celery	4	21	29	7
Cucumber	16	35	41	3
Eggplant	16	29	35	6
Endive		27		6
Kale		27		4
Kohlrabi		27		4
Leek		21		7
Lettuce	2	24	29	3
MuskMelon	16	32	38	4
Okra	16	35	41	6
Onion	2	24	35	6
Parsley	4	24	32	13
Parsnip	2	18	29	14
Pea	4	24	29	6
Pepper	16	29	35	8
Pumpkin	16	35	38	4
Radish	4	29	35	4
Rutabaga		27		4
Salsify		21		6
Spinach	2	21	29	5
Squash	16	35	38	4
Sweetcorn	10	35	41	3
Swiss Chard	4	29	35	4
Tomato	10	29	35	6
Turnip	4	29	41	3
WaterMelon	16	35	41	4

North India Growing Season

Plant	January	February	March	April	May	June	July	August	September	October	November	December
Tomato						■	■	■			■	■
Lettuce									■	■	■	
Spinach		■							■	■		
Cucumber		■	■			■	■					
Broccoli								■	■			
Cabbage									■	■		
Cauliflower						■	■		■	■		
Bottle Gourd		■	■			■	■					
Apple Gourd		■	■			■	■					
Bitter Gourd		■	■			■	■					
Capsicum	■				■	■					■	
Okra		■	■			■	■					
Peas										■	■	
Beans		■	■									
Carrot								■	■	■		
Melon		■	■			■	■					
Potato										■	■	■
Corn										■	■	
Radish	■								■	■	■	
Pumpkin	■	■				■	■					
Beetroot										■	■	
Turnip										■	■	
Onion					■	■	■					
Chillies							■	■		■	■	

South India Growing Season

Plant	January	February	March	April	May	June	July	August	September	October	November	December
Tomato	■	■				■				■	■	
Lettuce										■	■	■
Spinach									■	■		■
Cucumber	■					■	■		■			■
Broccoli								■	■		■	
Cabbage						■	■			■	■	
Cauliflower						■	■				■	
Bottle Gourd	■					■	■				■	■
Apple Gourd		■	■			■	■		■			
Bitter Gourd	■					■	■			■	■	
Capsicum	■				■	■			■	■	■	
Okra	■	■			■	■				■	■	■
Peas									■	■	■	■
Beans									■	■		
Carrot								■	■	■	■	■
Melon	■	■	■	■	■	■	■		■			
Potato										■	■	
Corn								■	■	■		
Radish									■	■		
Pumpkin	■					■	■					■
Beetroot								■	■	■	■	■
Turnip									■	■	■	
Onion			■	■		■	■	■	■	■		
Chillies				■	■							■

Commercial Hydroponics & Profits

Hydroponics is perhaps the only knowledge & business stream that offers ample opportunities to easily scale up the venture to any level practically, while benefiting humanity as well as the environment. Apart from being a perfect hobby, more importantly, hydroponics can be expanded from a hobby to any larger scale incrementally. What it means is that an individual practicing hobby-scale hydroponics can choose to keep expanding the scale in small steps as and when depending upon availability of space and capital. It's not a venture where one needs to devote time, effort & money to take the plethora of statutory approvals from the government – after all, it is horticulture, though constructing a polyhouse may require obtaining a permit and license. It's a venture where persons of any qualifications can be absorbed, obviating the need for skilled labor. The extent of labor involved is much less compared to conventional open field cultivation. The risk of destruction by pests is nearly eliminated, that's a big surety.

When taken at a commercial scale and if practiced right, hydroponics gives very good returns. Hydroponic produce commands a premium compared to usual open soil cultivation. The premium pricing of the hydroponic produce is not just because of the name *hydroponic*, but because of its inherent characteristics. Everything follows logic, so the price premium required by hydroponically produced veggies also has logical justifications. Justification and differentiators lie in the fact that hydroponically produced veggies generally have a better visual appeal, better size, better texture, balanced nutrition, wholesome flavor, are pesticide-free, and can be made available round the year with a steady supply. Hydroponic veggies can be produced closer to the cities where they are consumed, offering more freshness, consistent quality, and timely delivery.

Let's list down the differentiators to justify the price premium for hydroponically grown veggies compared to ordinary soil-grown veggies. These are the differentiators the commercial hydroponic must leverage to fetch a premium price for its produce:

- hydroponic veggies have a substantially better visual appeal and better texture.

- hydroponic veggies are generally better sized and fuller. Tomatoes & cucumbers are bigger and tighter, not pulpy. Leafy greens like Lettuce & Spinach have bigger and taut leaves.

- hydroponic veggies are more uniform in size & shape across the entire produce. You would generally not experience odd shapes and sizes of the produce.

- hydroponic veggies contain complete balanced nutrition, as per the natural constitution of that plant. That's because the nutrition supplied to the plant is balanced and complete, so is the completeness of nutrition with wholesome flavor in the hydroponic produce.

- hydroponic veggies do not contain any contaminants by accident. For example, soil might contain anything – lead, arsenic, or similar substances, which can get drawn into the produce. Nothing like that is possible in hydroponics, as its nutrition is controlled.

- hydroponic vegetables are generally pesticide-free.
- hydroponic vegetables can be made available year-round with a steady supply.

- hydroponic vegetables can be produced closer to the cities where they are consumed, offering more freshness, consistent quality, and timely delivery.

Observe carefully, aren't all the above-mentioned differentiators, the key characteristics most desired in the hotel & restaurant industry? The answer is, of course, Yes! That's where the opportunity for profit maximization lies. The hydroponic farmer should establish buying relationships with these bulk local consumers while setting up the commercial hydroponic venture. This is the way to extract maximum mileage and price benefit for the premium quality hydroponically produced goods emanating from one's hydroponic farm. It would not do justice to produce premium quality hydroponically grown goods and dump them in the open market next to the soil-grown veggies, as that would provide just some incremental pricing benefit. So, the strong recommendation is that the hydroponic entrepreneur should identify and establish long-term buying relationships with the local hotels & restaurants – to get maximum value for their premium produce. Hydroponically produced veggies offer the quality that must be capitalized on, a higher market price compared to ordinary soil-grown brethren, for multiplying the profits.

At commercial scale, it's important to focus on growing the plants that offer a premium. Growing hydroponic rice is possible but would be a disaster economically as the hydroponic rice would be much costlier to produce. Trying to market the hydroponic rice would become an all-involving project in itself, consuming all the available resources and in the process would take the venture into a nosedive. Why would anybody pay more for hydroponic rice? Growing veggies where freshness and quality can command a premium should be the objective. For these reasons, Lettuce, Basil, Herbs, Spinach, Pak Choy, Strawberries, Tomatoes and Cucumbers remain the top choices for commercial hydroponic growers. Hydroponically produced Cucumbers and Tomatoes look enticingly fresh and bigger, much sought after in the hotel

& restaurant industry. Lettuce, Basil, Herbs, Pak Choy, Spinach and Strawberries are seasonal in a soil-grown approach in an open environment but can be produced year-round in environment-controlled polyhouses.

The bottom line is to initiate one's commercial venture with Lettuce, Basil, Herbs, Spinach, Tomatoes, and Cucumbers only. Growing fodder is also a very good choice if you can establish its market. As the project matures and becomes stable, gradually diversify to grow more crops out of the many available choices. Capsicum, Chillies, and all other kinds of leafy vegetables could be the next good choice. Growing hydroponic flowers can be extremely profitable. Flowers like Gerbera, Chrysanthemum, Orchid, and Carnations are always in high demand in the flower industry but can be grown in suitable low-temperature zones only. Hydroponics offers the opportunity to grow these flowers round the year in climate-controlled polyhouses and can be very profitable owing to the high pricing of flowers in the market. Commercial hydroponic growers also grow exotic fruit plants like Blueberries, Raspberries, and Cranberries – but that requires a bit more care in maintaining climate control. Fruit plants like Watermelons, Muskmelon, and Cantaloupe can be grown quite well through the hydroponic technique, where opportunities exist in the local market.

For practicing commercial hydroponics, constructing a climate-controlled polyhouse is essential, so it becomes necessary to have a fair understanding of the options and costs involved, as presented hereafter.

To create a controlled environment, there needs to be an enclosure.

An enclosure, when made of bricks and mortar – like normal buildings, would be extremely expensive.

Enclosures of earlier days were built of glass and polycarbonate – called glasshouses, which have high strength and allow for proofing the enclosure for very effective air-conditioning.

However, the construction of a glasshouse is extremely expensive, and hardly 5% of commercial growers would opt for this.

Enclosures made of a sturdy pipe framework and covered with UV-stabilized polyfilm sheets are called polyhouses and offer the cheapest way to create an enclosure… a Low-Cost Greenhouse Solution. Pest control is also easy to maintain in the polyhouses generally. A polyhouse is a structure that insulates the internal environment from outside weather, thus providing an environment conducive for growing plants.

The most basic polyhouse is a small tunnel-type construction, just about a meter high. A polyhouse tunnel shields the plants from rain and direct sunrays while allowing filtered light to pass through. Polyhouse tunnels are installed in parallel with a walking galley in between and can be improvised to supply cold air from its open side to keep the inside temperature low. Polyhouse tunnels do not have a strong framework and may get displaced or collapse in high winds. It's generally not the choice of construction in hydroponics due to the difficulty of using it, though popular in soil-based cultivation. It's the cheapest, costing just about Rs 600 (7 USD) per sq. meter (year 2024).

A polyhouse made using a sturdy framework of galvanized iron (GI) pipes or tubes, with a meter-deep foundation to support and anchor it to the ground, is the polyhouse most used in commercial hydroponic establishments. It is well-driven into the ground to prevent it from collapsing in high winds or heavy rain. It is covered by UV-stabilized polyfilm sheets, which are stretched and become very firm to withstand high winds and rain. These polyhouses are typically 3 meters high, and other dimensions can be anything as per requirement. They can be built as required, ranging from small structures suitable for home gardens to large commercial levels. The bigger the construction, the lower the cost per square meter in general. Such polyhouses can be installed in all kinds of weather conditions, particularly useful in states where harsh high temperatures up to 45 degrees Celsius with high winds might prevail in some months.

The polyfilm has to be necessarily UV-stabilized so that it remains unaffected in direct sun. UV stabilization of the polyfilm prevents it from disintegrating or cracking after prolonged use in direct sun. Polyfilms can easily remain intact for more than 5 years in use when UV-stabilized 200-micron diffused polyethylene sheets are used. Higher quality sheets can last even up to 10 years. The higher the micron of the polyfilm, the higher its strength. The higher the UV grade of the polyfilm, the longer its life.

Polyhouses are usually dome-shaped constructions. Flat roof constructions are also available, but they offer less protection from rain apart from having lesser roof strength. Flat roof constructions are cheaper compared to dome-shaped constructions but have issues and a lower lifespan.

It is possible to construct the polyhouse using even cheap bamboo poles, but they won't be durable, nor would they be able to offer strength. Polyfilms on such cheap bamboo hut-type structures would tear away due to the uneven surface of bamboo poles. Such basic structures can indeed be fitted with air fans for somewhat climate control, but in the long run, such structures would prove more expensive compared to a regular polyhouse. That's due to their low life. These are the type that may be considered for hydroponics only if the location where one is operating does not require climate control and shielding from direct sun & rain is the sole objective at a very low-cost.

Choosing a polyhouse with a galvanized iron or aluminum framework is the minimum that the professional hydroponic grower should consider. A polyhouse allows the user to control the climate inside, depending on the extent of equipment used for the purpose. A polyhouse can be of 2 types: Naturally Ventilated or Environmentally Controlled Polyhouse.

A naturally ventilated polyhouse is just a structure with minimum equipment inside. Air flow is maintained by opening the ventilators and air ingress doors. The underlying principle is that the hot air would rise toward the top of the polyhouse, where ventilator doors are provided to let the hot air out, thereby maintaining natural air circulation. For temperature control, misting devices called foggers are provided that also increase the humidity, though. At a minimum, every polyhouse would need to have the basic humidity controller. As the plants grow, they transpire through their leaves, losing water in the form of vapor into the surrounding ambiance. That's the main reason for the humidity to keep rising within the polyhouse, necessitating humidity controllers that would switch on/off the ventilator exhausts.

Environmentally Controlled Polyhouse is a more sophisticated type of polyhouse. These are equipped with air fans and pad systems for proper air temperature control. Operation of Fan and Pad systems inside polyhouses is quite similar to the evaporative type of air coolers quite ubiquitous in Asian countries. Pads are kept moist with water, while the fans pull air through those moist pads to cool the air by the evaporative effect of water. Depending on the length of the polyhouse, a series of air fans are provided that pull moist & cooled air from one side of the polyhouse and send it out through its other end. Fan and Pad systems sufficiently cool down the temperatures as per the requirements of hydroponics. An issue with the Fan and Pad systems is that they increase the humidity inside the polyhouse – which is actually fine for plants. But if the plants one is growing require humidity to be lowered, humidity control requires vapor compression-type air-conditioning and that immediately jacks up the cost substantially. It's not cheap to air condition the vast expanse of the polyhouse and should be considered only as the very last addition if really required by the plants one is growing. For example, if the intention is to grow exotic and expensive plants like strawberries that require low-humidity, that can well justify the cost of air-conditioning. Polyhouses are generally equipped with thermostats to manage the temperatures inside, but opening or closing the exhausts and by starting or switching off the fans that also help control the humidity to the required extent.

Polyhouses don't come cheap.

The cheapest type of polyhouse would be the narrow tunnel-type polyhouse, just about a meter high, that can be constructed for just Rs 600 (7 USD) per square meter in the year 2024. But these are not for hydroponics.

A naturally ventilated polyhouse generally costs around Rs. 1500 (17 USD) per square meter for a construction of 1000 square meters – which usually suffices for most hydroponic needs. Costs vary depending on the strength and quality of the material used.

When Fan and Pad systems are added with humidity controllers, the cost would typically be in the range of Rs 2500 (28 USD) per square meter for a construction of 1000 square meters.

If sophisticated automation and some air-conditioning are added to the polyhouse, the installation cost would further increase by at least RsRs 1500 (17 USD) per square meter, though it can be less or more depending on the type of sophistication.

Construction of a glass or polycarbonate glasshouse is prohibitively expensive and can be justified only in places where the hydroponic produce can command a super high premium.

Installation cost is not the only cost that should drive the choices in commercial hydroponics. It would be worthwhile to elaborate on the associated costs that can make-or-break the venture.

Cost of water

Generally, groundwater has high hardness and requires investment in reverse osmosis (RO) systems to remove that hardness. If the person plans to install the hydroponic set-up where a borewell needs to be drilled to extract groundwater, it is nearly certain that the set-up will require a significant investment in an RO system with water storage and pumping. However, if the hydroponic set-up is located where river water is available in the vicinity, that will reduce the investment in RO considerably. That's because river water is generally soft with a hardness level not exceeding 100-150. The higher the hardness in water, the higher the hardness removal cost. Selecting the location of one's hydroponic set-up closer to a river source would reduce set-up and operating costs. Municipal water is also generally soft as it comes from river water or after desalination.

An associated aspect is that during rains, water accumulation on the site can be a problem. Choose a site where waterlogging during monsoons is not an issue.

Cost of air temperature

Compared to locating the hydroponic set-up in hot zones, it would serve better to locate them where the air temperature remains generally low throughout the year. It's for this reason that Bengaluru and its surroundings are favored for installing hydroponic setups.

Cost of humidity

In locations where the humidity in the air remains generally high regularly, the Fan and Pad systems will not work, as these systems cool air through the evaporation of water. But if the air is already saturated with water, evaporative type fan & pad systems do not provide the cooling effect. Such places will necessitate an investment in expensive vapor compression-type air-conditioning systems, thereby escalating the cost. Generally, this is a factor that gets overlooked by hydroponic entrepreneurs.

Cost of transport

It is imperative to locate the hydroponic setups closer to the market so that the hydroponic produce can reach the end users fast enough to preserve the freshness and quality. Cities are the major consumers of hydroponic produce, thereby making it essential to locate the set-up within the vicinity of cities to reduce transport costs.

Cost of light

Setting up multi-tiered systems within the polyhouse may require the addition of artificial lights to provide good coverage to the plants. Grow lights are expensive and require electricity to run. When setting up the system design, the focus should be to maximize the utilization of sunlight coming in diffused via the polyfilm.

Cost of electricity

Hydroponic setups require air pumps and water pumps to circulate the hydroponic solution and to keep it oxygenated. Running the fans and lights consumes additional electricity. At the end of the month, the electricity bill will not be small and would hurt. Installation of solar panels can be a worthwhile investment to be considered along with the installation of hydroponic polyhouses.

Cost of Labor

Hydroponics requires labor. Saplings need to be grown from seeds, then each net pot needs to be planted carefully with saplings and fixed to the hydroponic system. Nutrients need to be prepared. Water top-up needs to be done. pH needs to be monitored, and pH Down/Up solutions need to be dosed. Hydroponic produce needs to be harvested every day and packaged. All these jobs can be performed using unskilled or semi-skilled labor but require hands, nevertheless.

Automation

Keeping a constant watch over all the parameters is not something that requires 100% devotion or attention. Checking the parameters once every 2-3 days is sufficient. It would take hardly an hour to check all parameters like pH, TDS, humidity, solution temperature, and air temperature. If the check can be performed once a day, even better, as it can avoid the cost of any kind of automation. Some over-zealous growers go overboard by installing all kinds of online sensors - pH, TDS, temperatures, humidity - and connect them for live streaming to their computers and phones! That's going overboard; it is not that the plants would suddenly change these parameters within minutes. Changes would be slow, gradual, and occasional readings are adequate. Lots of automation technology would be necessary for growing hydroponic plants in space by NASA, but not essential for ground-based hydroponics.

State Government Subsidies

Several state governments incentivize setting up of polyhouses by contributing as much as 50 percent of the installed cost. That can be a very significant boost, as all entrepreneurs face cash crunches to start with. Checking if the local government offers such a policy should be the first thing to do before finalizing any location for polyhouses.

Cost of Land

Setting up a hydroponic venture does not require investment in prime commercial land. The market for the produce being in cities, it's logical to locate the hydroponic set-up in the vicinity of the city, but it's not required to be on prime land. Renting agricultural land in the vicinity of cities, like suburbs, is surprisingly cheap. For example, it is possible to rent one full acre of agricultural land for just one lakh rupees (USD 1100) per year close to Gurugram. That hardly impacts the economics. Buying the agricultural land is another matter, as buying it doesn't come cheap. So, just go for rental.

Type of system

This aspect has earlier been discussed in detail in the earlier sections. Selecting a complicated system that requires high expertise and maintenance may prove counterproductive. Selecting a vertical growing system may appear to be space-saving, allowing the growth of multiple layers of crops in the same space, but it requires careful installation to allow light to fall on all the plants, apart from access issues. Vertical installation would need adequate access corridors to move the ladders around and requires labor to go up and down the ladders to manage upper tiers. Aeroponics systems would have their spray nozzles choked often, requiring maintenance. NFT systems can be used for small plants only like spinach, parsley, coriander, lettuce, etc., that do not require trellis support as the plant height is small. DWC systems would require high aeration but are most recommended due to low maintenance and cost.

Typically, NFT systems with a climate-controlled polyhouse would cost nearly Rs one crore to 1.5 crore (USD 110,000 – 165,000) per acre in the year 2024 in India, though the cost changes depending on the type of equipment and arrangement of the system (horizontal/vertical) and the use of lights. With DWC systems, the overall cost would reduce by approximately 25%. Media bed systems would be even cheaper, cutting the cost further by about 20 percent. Aeroponic systems, on the other hand, would increase the cost.

Evidently, the polyhouse cost is the predominant cost for hydroponic systems. Looking at it another way, for an NFT farm, the polyhouse cost can be 50% of the total cost. For DWC, the polyhouse cost would be 70% of the total cost. For media bed systems, the polyhouse cost would be 90% of the total installation cost.

Polyhouses are an excellent means to practice commercial hydroponics in climate-controlled environments, as the polyfilm provides a barrier that excludes the external environment and enables the internal environment to be controlled. Polyhouses enable a person to engage in year-round cultivation and to grow veggies irrespective of the season. Polyhouses allow a person to adjust temperature, humidity, light, and air. Polyhouses are indeed an enabler and a boon for commercial hydroponics, providing affordability and efficiency simultaneously.

High installation cost, particularly of the polyhouses, is the main factor that serves as the bottleneck for starting a commercial hydroponic venture. In this regard, the budding entrepreneur should apply mind and consider what ingenuity can be brought in to harness the escalating cost. Hydroponics is all about innovation, and that does not get limited to equipment suppliers only. Budding entrepreneurs may think of converting unused basements of buildings for hydroponics – as they anyway remain cool and with minimum improvisation can be turned into climate-controlled enclosures fit for hydroponic cultivation. Using basements of buildings would require using artificial grow lights; nevertheless, for which the installation of solar panel can be considered to couple with the basement lights. This is not popular currently but holds immense potential as the cost of solar panels has nosedived, making them very affordable. There may be an oversupply of unused commercial buildings in some metropolitan cities like Gurugram, with their vast underground parking lying unused. Can these be used for hydroponics, instead of buying/renting land and then constructing a polyhouse on it – should be explored by budding hydroponic entrepreneurs.

Before rushing headlong into installing a polyhouse, an entrepreneur should evaluate all the aforementioned points and then make a careful decision to ensure the viability and success of the commercial hydroponic venture.

The following pages present the most important aspect of all: COSTING and PROFITS.

These comparisons will help exhibit the cost and profit differences between various commercial setups for hydroponic ventures. Read them carefully. These are realistic figures as of the year 2024. Accordingly, apply the inflation depending on when you are reading it.

These case studies consider growing Lettuce, that easily commands selling price of Rupees 20 – 30 (0.2 USD) per head in India in wholesale. These Case studies consider conservative selling price of Rupees 20 (0.2 USD) per head.

'Payback' means the time you can expect for your investment to return to you.

Case-1

Multi-tier NFT, with Grow lights			
Type of Polyhouse	**Fan & Pad**		
Plant	Lettuce		
Total plot space	2,000	m2	
LxB of each module	3m x 1m		
Number of modules	400		
Number of Tiers	3	In each module	
Number of plants	300	In each module	
Total number of plants	1,20,000		
Power for lights, PER MONTH	11,34,000	INR	12600 USD
Nutrient, PER MONTH	1,35,000	INR	1500 USD
Labour, PER MONTH	80,000	INR	889 USD
Seeds	1,20,000	INR	1333 USD
Other costs, per month	1,20,000	INR	1333 USD
Selling price per plant	20	INR	0.2 USD
Revenue PER MONTH	24,00,000	INR	26667 USD
Profit PER MONTH	8,11,000	INR	9011 USD
Profit PER YEAR	97,32,000	INR	108133 USD
Investment (Approx)	1,60,00,000	INR	177778 USD
Payback	1.6	years	

This system is most often used by commercial growers. This one is on half acre of land with polyhouse, with NFT modules inside coupled with Grow lights. Grow lights are expensive to install and to run. Being multi-tiered, installation of Grow lights is imperative. Grow lights provide the speed of growth and the assured continuity – important in commercial hydroponics. This system has payback of 1.6 years.

Next, let's see how the payback changes when multi-tier system is changed to single tier.

Case-2

Single-tier NFT, No Grow lights			
Type of Polyhouse	**Fan & Pad**		
Plant	Lettuce		
Total plot space	2,000	m2	
LxB of each module	3m x 1m		
Number of modules	400		
Number of Tiers	1	In each module	
Number of plants	100	In each module	
Total number of plants	40,000		
Power for lights, PER MONTH	-	INR	0 USD
Nutrient, PER MONTH	45,000	INR	500 USD
Labour, PER MONTH	40,000	INR	444 USD
Seeds	40,000	INR	444 USD
Other costs, per month	40,000	INR	444 USD
Selling price per plant	20	INR	0.2 USD
Revenue PER MONTH	8,00,000	INR	8889 USD
Profit PER MONTH	6,35,000	INR	7056 USD
Profit PER YEAR	76,20,000	INR	84667 USD
Investment (Approx)	89,00,000	INR	98889 USD
Payback	1.2	years	

Being single tier NFT system, installation of Grow lights is not essential, as all the plants can capture sunlight filtering in from top and sides. Reduced structure due to single tier, and without Grow lights, the payback reduces to 1.2 years. This is also a large installation, on half acre land.

Next, we see what happens if we grow small, on just 100 square meters of land.

Case-3

Single-tier NFT, No Grow lights			
Type of Polyhouse	**Fan & Pad**		
Plant	Lettuce		
Total plot space	100	m2	
LxB of each module	3m x 1m		
Number of modules	20		
Number of Tiers	1	In each module	
Number of plants	100	In each module	
Total number of plants	2,000		
Power for lights, PER MONTH	-	INR	0 USD
Nutrient, PER MONTH	2,250	INR	25 USD
Labour, PER MONTH	20,000	INR	222 USD
Seeds	2,000	INR	22 USD
Other costs, per month	2,000	INR	22 USD
Selling price per plant	20	INR	0.2 USD
Revenue PER MONTH	40,000	INR	444 USD
Profit PER MONTH	13,750	INR	153 USD
Profit PER YEAR	1,65,000	INR	1833 USD
Investment (Approx)	4,45,000	INR	4944 USD
Payback	2.7	years	

Because this system is small - on just 100 square meters of land, payback jumps up to 2.7 years. This is what most newbies attempt to do and find the payback is not in line with expectation - causing disillusionment. In American or European setups, scales are huge and so is the profitability.

Now, if someone wants to improve profitability of this small system itself, what to do ? A solution is on next page – with Naturally ventilated polyhouse instead of Fan & Pad system.

Case-4

Single-tier NFT, No Grow lights			
Type of Polyhouse	**Naturally ventilated**		
Plant	Lettuce		
Total plot space	100	m2	
LxB of each module	3m x 1m		
Number of modules	20		
Number of Tiers	1	In each module	
Number of plants	100	In each module	
Total number of plants	2,000		
Power for lights, PER MONTH	-	INR	0 USD
Nutrient, PER MONTH	2,250	INR	25 USD
Labour, PER MONTH	20,000	INR	222 USD
Seeds	2,000	INR	22 USD
Other costs, per month	2,000	INR	22 USD
Selling price per plant	20	INR	0.2 USD
Revenue PER MONTH	40,000	INR	444 USD
Profit PER MONTH	13,750	INR	153 USD
Profit PER YEAR	1,65,000	INR	1833 USD
Investment (Approx)	3,45,000	INR	3833 USD
Payback	2.1	years	

Here, in the small setup of just 100 square meters, payback improves to 2.1 years by using the naturally ventilated polyhouse.

But didn't we mention payback being just one year initially in the book ? Let's get there next.

Case-5

Single-tier DWC, No Grow lights			
Type of Polyhouse	**Fan & Pad**		
Plant	Lettuce		
Total plot space	2,000	m2	
LxB of each module	3m x 1m		
Number of modules	400		
Number of Tiers	1	In each module	
Number of plants	100	In each module	
Total number of plants	40,000		
Power for lights, PER MONTH	-	INR	0 USD
Nutrient, PER MONTH	45,000	INR	500 USD
Labour, PER MONTH	40,000	INR	444 USD
Seeds	40,000	INR	444 USD
Other costs, per month	40,000	INR	444 USD
Selling price per plant	20	INR	0.2 USD
Revenue PER MONTH	8,00,000	INR	8889 USD
Profit PER MONTH	6,35,000	INR	7056 USD
Profit PER YEAR	76,20,000	INR	84667 USD
Investment (Approx)	76,00,000	INR	84444 USD
Payback	1.0	years	

This is the DWC system, that I most recommend, but its least advertised because it does not have much equipment in it for the manufacturers to sell. This setup is also on half acre of land on which polyhouse if constructed, with DWC modules inside. Because it's a single tier system, it does not have Grow lights. Adding Grow lights will increase the speed of growth, with assured continuity of produce – but will increase payback. This system has payback of 1 year. Depending upon the consistent availability of sunlight, the speed of growth might vary, and to account for that consider real payback slightly more as 1.2 years.

Next let's see how the payback changes with Naturally ventilated polyhouse instead of Fan & Pad system.

Case-6

Single-tier DWC, No Grow lights			
Type of Polyhouse	**Naturally ventilated**		
Plant	Lettuce		
Total plot space	2,000	m2	
LxB of each module	3m x 1m		
Number of modules	400		
Number of Tiers	1	In each module	
Number of plants	100	In each module	
Total number of plants	40,000		
Power for lights, PER MONTH	-	INR	0 USD
Nutrient, PER MONTH	45,000	INR	500 USD
Labour, PER MONTH	40,000	INR	444 USD
Seeds	40,000	INR	444 USD
Other costs, per month	40,000	INR	444 USD
Selling price per plant	20	INR	0.2 USD
Revenue PER MONTH	8,00,000	INR	8889 USD
Profit PER MONTH	6,35,000	INR	7056 USD
Profit PER YEAR	76,20,000	INR	84667 USD
Investment (Approx)	56,00,000	INR	62222 USD
Payback	0.7	years	

With Naturally ventilated polyhouse instead of Fan & Pad system in DWC system, payback reduces even further to just 0.7 years. Depending upon the consistent availability of sunlight, the speed of growth might vary, and to account for that, consider real payback slightly more at 0.9 year.

Case-7

Single-tier DWC, With Grow lights			
Type of Polyhouse	**Fan & Pad**		
Plant	Lettuce		
Total plot space	2,000	m2	
LxB of each module	3m x 1m		
Number of modules	400		
Number of Tiers	1	In each module	
Number of plants	100	In each module	
Total number of plants	40,000		
Power for lights, PER MONTH	3,78,000	INR	4200 USD
Nutrient, PER MONTH	45,000	INR	500 USD
Labour, PER MONTH	40,000	INR	444 USD
Seeds	40,000	INR	444 USD
Other costs, PER MONTH	40,000	INR	444 USD
Selling price per plant	20	INR	0.2 USD
Revenue PER MONTH	8,00,000	INR	8889 USD
Profit PER MONTH	2,57,000	INR	2856 USD
Profit PER YEAR	30,84,000	INR	34267 USD
Investment (Approx)	91,00,000	INR	101111 USD
Payback	3.0	years	

Here, Grow lights are added to the DWC system inside polyhouse with Fan & Pad system, and payback jumps up to 3 years – simply due to the addition of GrowLights.

With all these case studies, reader can hopefully now make an informed decision.

A point to make here is that the cost of rental of the land is not factored in the aforementioned case studies. The reason for that is the rental cost of agricultural land is not high. Hydroponics does not necessarily require commercial prime land. Renting agricultural land in city suburbs is surprisingly cheap. For example, it is possible to rent one full acre of agricultural land for just one lakh rupees (USD 1100) per year close to Gurugram. That's a minor impact to the economics.

Some new insights gained through these case studies :

- As you keep increasing the scale of operations, better would become the profitability. Smaller the operation, lesser would be its profitability. Small operations are good to get practical understanding of affairs, but to make good profit, go big.

- Investment in Grow lights is the biggest make or break factor. Try to avoid them if possible and rely more on sunlight. Consider investing in Solar power – that can be a very significant profit contributor. Cost of electricity gets negated by the free solar power, but requires investment. Shed that supports the solar panels, becomes the roof of your polyhouse – just needing to shield it from sides – so polyhouse cost goes down. Government subsidies are available for solar installations. This should be considered by prospective hydroponic growers.

- Stay with DWC or NFT systems. These are reliable and hassle-free operation.

- Stay with exotic veggies – Lettuce, Basil, Spinach, Herbs, Pak Choy, Tomatoes, Cucumbers – that fetch high price and remain in demand with hotels and restaurants.

- Cost of buying land can be exorbitant. Stay away from buying land. Rental of agricultural land in city vicinity is surprisingly cheap, so go for that. There's no need to rent any prime land as that will eat away the profits. Keep the rental cost of land low, as hydroponic setups can be built by renting that very dirt cheap land that no one wants.

It is possible to do hydroponics for super exotic plants also – like saffron and medicinal plants. There are people who are already doing hydroponic saffron in India, raking in good money. Payback of such ventures would be astonishingly lower, but requires very specific care and direct experience of growing that kind of plant. That may be the next step to venture into.

Marketing your Hydroponic Produce

Unless it's sold, it's useless. Revenue is the key in any business venture, so it is in a hydroponic venture as well. Hydroponic produce has its own distinguishers that need to be leveraged to maximize the returns. Placing the hydroponic produce next to the soil-grown produce would yield little profits, if any. Hydroponic produce always commands a premium, and the hydroponic growers need to market its distinct distinguishers.

Hydroponic produce can offer exotic veggies and herbs year-round, something unlikely through the open soil-grown route.

Hydroponic produce is visually more appealing, with the veggies being more shapely and vibrant due to the balanced nutrition they thrive in.

Hydroponic produce is mostly pesticide-free. That's because most plant diseases originate from soil, and soil is absent in hydroponics. Only airborne diseases might come, which can be handled well by organic neem spray. Commercial growers sometimes release ladybirds in their polyhouse, and each ladybird can eat 200-400 eggs every day – obviating the need for even neem spray.

Hydroponic produce can be harvested year-round, providing supply assurance to customers.

Hydroponic produce in polyhouses remains insulated from extreme weather elements, which, again, assures the continuity of supply.

Hydroponic produce can offer consistent pricing due to its remaining unaffected by weather events. For example, tomato prices fluctuate between Rs 20 to Rs 150 per kg in India, but hydroponic produce will come to the customer at steady pricing.

Hydroponic produce can reach its customers faster, as these farms are generally in the vicinity of consumers.

All the above are of paramount importance in the gourmet restaurants and hotels, where these differentiators matter. For that reason, restaurants and hotels are willing to purchase high-quality hydroponic produce at a premium. Start by researching the local market to identify the most suitable plants that suit the local restaurants and hotels. Visit local markets, including grocery stores, specialty food shops, and farmers' markets. Observe what herbs they currently offer and assess their freshness. One would generally be surprised by the poor condition of "fresh" herbs on offer, and there lies the opportunity. Observe the prices, sizing of the 'bunch', and the packaging formats. Observe how the markets are storing the fresh products on shelves; that'll decide the sturdiness of packaging that you would be using. While exploring the market, investigate the quantities being sold. Are certain herbs more popular than others? Compile findings from various small markets and organize this information to determine what kinds of leafy produce are selling well and at what price points. Some of the perpetually best-selling herbs remain Basil, Cilantro, Parsley, Thyme, Rosemary.

Rather than competing with everyone else, seek out unique opportunities by interviewing restaurant and market owners, or even the local flower market. Fresh cut flowers that are used in bouquets are a very good venture, but breaking into that market requires ingenuity and can be challenging. Flowers also take longer to grow compared to herbs. Herbs are fast-growing. Basil, in particular, remains in high demand in metro restaurants. Hydroponic basil is easy and fast to grow, with bigger leaves compared to soil-grown. Tomatoes and peppers are also perpetually in demand, but take longer to grow compared to herbs, lettuce, and spinach.

The hydroponic market is growing at a good pace. Chances are that once you have established your hydroponic set-up and the market, others would follow in the vicinity itself. But it would take time for others to catch up with the experience, and your know-how would remain the differentiator as the copycats would not have invested time reading this book as carefully as you have, nor would have the experience that you would have gained. Use that experience and know-how to keep improving your reliability. Reliability regarding the quality of produce, and reliability regarding the continuity of produce are 2 important aspects you would have gained ahead of others. Quality and consistency are of paramount importance in hydroponics. As experience builds up, hydroponic growers generally open up parallel markets by exporting their produce, which brings stability to the venture. As you keep increasing the scale of operations, profitability would improve, as would be evident in a few case studies presented just in the preceding pages.

While starting up, do not invest in getting high-quality custom packaging. Custom packaging doesn't come cheap and requires a minimum lot size. Keeping the working capital relatively free should be a priority. Many growers start off by getting their custom-made plastic and cardboard packaging in bulk, requiring it to be stored well, consuming real estate apart from locking the capital. Avoid unnecessary expenses to begin with. Go with readily available off-the-shelf plastic packaging and cardboard boxes. Use a hole punch to create 'breathing' holes in the bags, ensuring product freshness. Before sealing the bags, lightly mist your herbs with water. Weigh your herbs using a small weighing scale to maintain uniformity across packages. For perishable soft produce like lettuce, it would do good to package them in secondary hard cardboard packaging. A well-designed package can make a significant difference in how customers perceive your fresh produce.

Get only your brand stickers made, which can be pasted onto the off-the-shelf packaging. Branding your produce with your own logo and particulars gives assurance to the customers, and they know what to look for in repeat purchases. Building your own brand allows you to establish recognition and credibility.

Differentiate yourself by positioning yourself as a conscientious grower who uses only the finest nutrients and purest water. Emphasize that your herbs are free from harmful chemicals like insecticides, fungicides, and herbicides. This commitment to quality will sway customers toward your produce over field-grown alternatives of uncertain origin. A thoughtful approach and attention to detail can set you apart in the competitive market. Consider inserting a small business card with every package that serves as a professional touchpoint should the customer wish to inquire or get into a direct regular purchase agreement.

Summary Critical points for hydroponics

Temperature

If the temperature of the hydroponic solution becomes more than 20-25 degrees C, then that adversely impacts the nutrient-absorbing capability of the roots. Plastic exposed to direct sun gets very hot, and that heats up the hydroponic solution. So, if using plastic, make provisions to prevent its direct exposure to the sun. Covering plastic pipes with aluminum foil helps. As long as the hydroponic solution temperature is kept below 25 degrees C or so, high ambient air temperature can be sustained by plants. On hot sunny days, shade the outdoor hydroponic system. Doing outdoor hydroponics in peak summer is difficult.

TDS

TDS is the most important measuring parameter in hydroponics. It's directly linked to EC (Electrical Conductivity), so there's no need to check EC separately. TDS measurement is important.

pH

The optimum pH range for hydroponics is 4 to 6.5.

A lower pH is not much of an issue.

pH more than 6.5 is NOT good. Use 'pH DOWN' to lower it.

Air

Roots need air. This is very important to prevent root decay. Use an air pump to introduce air into the hydroponic solution. It is not necessary to keep the air pump always on. It can be switched on in the morning during daytime and switched off at night.

Nutrients

Use the best quality nutrients. It's a small cost compared to the overall hydroponic cost.

Do not put too much quantity of nutrients. Higher amounts of nutrients can cause reverse osmosis in the roots. Use half-strength most of the time and you may use full-strength during the flowering/fruiting stage.

Root Zone Space

Roots need space to grow. The more root zone space, the better. Try to select hydroponic systems that provide good vertical root zone height for roots to grow. Tomato plants would require at least 8-10 inches of vertical root zone space to grow well. Lettuce can thrive in just a 2-inch space.

Light

Leaves need light, and sunlight is the best as long as it doesn't scorch the leaves. At least 3-4 hours of light every day. The more light, the more the growth.

Seeds

Always use fresh and good-quality seeds. Do not compromise on seeds. Avoid using seeds left over from last season. Try to buy seeds from local seed/fertilizer shops, as they usually keep in-season & fresh seeds and provide free growing tips along with. Buying seeds from good online stores is also fine. Sow seeds in moistened coco peat and expose them to the sun. Humidity and warmth are both important to grow seeds into saplings.

Saplings

Buying saplings directly from the local nursery is a good idea. It saves time to grow them. Wash the roots gently, and then transplant them in net pots.

Humidity

Very low-humidity will dry the leaves and restrict plant growth. High humidity is not as much of an issue for most plants.

Volume of Hydroponic Solution

Keep a large volume of hydroponic solution. The more, the better, as it provides consistency of TDS. Keep at least 1-2 liters of hydroponic solution per leafy plant. For vines, keep at least 5-6 liters of hydroponic solution per plant.

Pollination

If the hydroponic system is placed where bees or moths cannot reach, how will flowers get pollinated?

So, keep your hydroponic system in the open for flowering plants. Indoors is okay for leafy plants, but not for fruiting plants.

When doing indoor hydroponics in closed environments, people need to use a brush to cross-pollinate the flowers. For tomato plants, shaking the plants helps in self-pollination of flowers.

Algae

If the hydroponic solution is exposed to sunlight, then algae will develop quickly in the hydroponic solution. Always shield the hydroponic solution from sunlight. Painting the hydroponic system dark is beneficial. Covering all holes is advisable so that light does not seep in through the open holes.

Chapter 5

Mysteries of Environment

It was in the year 2018 when I was conversing with a friend. I told him, "Sidhu, do you know… you can grow plants without soil – that's the hydroponics technique."

He retorted, "Why bother? Just put them in soil and they'll grow."

Sidhu is known in our friend circle for his no-nonsense approach to life.

Practical, pragmatic. No complications.

That's how he manages his thriving commercial enterprise, employing hundreds.

We were conversing in his house that has gardens on all sides – where he practices a kitchen garden. That's what started this conversation where I asked him if he had heard of hydroponics. It took less than 5 minutes for me to explain it briefly to him, and that got him interested to try it out. Soon he had his terrace filled with hydroponic setups and is now a prolific hydroponics.

Why do some people have a stronger propensity to try out new things?

A study was conducted by Prof. Richard Wiseman, a psychologist by profession, sometime toward the start of this century, and he published an interesting study called 'The Luck Factor'. Richard conducted a practical to understand why some people consider themselves lucky while others do not. A sample of about 4 hundred persons was gathered at a venue and divided into 2 groups – people who considered themselves 'lucky' and those who considered themselves 'not-so-lucky'. Everyone was given a newspaper and asked to tell how many photographs were inside. Mostly, the unlucky people went on counting the photographs throughout the entire newspaper, while most lucky people were able to notice the huge texts that stood out and declared, "*Stop counting – There are 43 photographs in this newspaper*" and again after a few pages "*Stop counting, tell the experimenter you have seen this and win $250.*" These messages were printed too big and bold to be missed - with texts 2 inches tall. But the unlucky people generally missed it, and the lucky people generally spotted it.

The point here is that the people who considered themselves 'not-so-lucky' were generally narrow-minded and fixated. They focused ONLY on the photos in this case, as was told, and totally neglected to observe the associated text.

On the other hand, people who considered themselves 'lucky' had an open vision. While looking for photos, they kept their mind open to other possibilities... i.e., text in this case.

There was only one thing that separated the lucky and unlucky people from each other — their behavior, emanating from their thought process.

Keeping oneself open to the existence of lateral possibilities is one way to be lucky.

If this experiment is to be taken at its face value, a logical conclusion that may be drawn is that it's in our own hands to be lucky or not! Luck is not something that a person has to be born with necessarily, though that may also be true. Being lucky is something that one can cultivate by keeping an open mind and being receptive to the lateral associated possibilities that continually keep crossing one's path while traversing this life circle. Luck may not necessarily be a mystical charm that few are born with; rather, it can also be an outcome of having a welcoming attitude toward alternatives.

In this experiment, one can also deduce that the people who consider themselves lucky are more open to taking risks and thereby bolder by nature, making true the maxim 'Luck favors the bold'.

Why I recalled this study here is to emphasize the fact that it's up to us to make ourselves lucky or unlucky. We have to be open to lateral vision and alternatives to explore in life. It helps to open new channels in life. If you like greens and love gardening, then it would make sense to have an open mind and try out hydroponics – where you can really see the plants grow on a daily basis. In hydroponics, an increase in plant size can be visible on a daily basis – something that's not possible in conventional gardening. And of course, its commercial applications are tantalisingly favorable.

My friend Sidhu had listened to me with an open mind and was open to trying out new ideas, open to exploration.

This attitude opened a parallel channel for him, and now he has doubled the avenues of his joys.

One experiment is just what it is, an experiment. One lucky experiment can be a fluke and should not suffice to believe a life-changing point. Prof. Wiseman conducted numerous experiments and interviews with hundreds of people with diverse backgrounds - a retired accountant, a nurse, a salesman, a flight attendant, etc., to eliminate the possibility of having uniformity in thinking cultivated through likeness in professional lives. Results supported the thought process that lucky people are more receptive to trying out newer things, while the persons who consider themselves unlucky are generally more cautious, fixated, and rigid, favoring paths that would be less risky. Prof. Wiseman published many more experiments in his book 'The Luck Factor', suggesting, *"Lucky people are more relaxed and open, and therefore see what is there rather than just what they are looking for."*

Prof. Wiseman went ahead and demonstrated the transformative application of his luck theory in real-life. He created the 'Luck School' – a series of experiments where he designed some techniques and educated his people in these techniques - enabling people to think and behave like lucky individuals. The techniques were generally aimed at educating people about how to break daily routines and seize the lateral opportunities that might otherwise pass by, or how to examine a bad happening with a lens that also reimagines how it could have been worse. Just after a month of practicing those techniques, people reported more satisfaction in life and felt 'luckier' in all walks of their lives.

Experiments apart, consider this real-life scenario. Suppose a person lives near an apple orchard and goes out to pluck some apples every day to meet their needs. The person would tend to pluck the apples from trees located close by, to reduce their efforts of gathering the few apples needed. Over time, due to repeated plucking of apples from the same trees in the vicinity, the availability of apples would become dearer with every passing day. If the person continues to visit the same earlier trees over and over again, chances are that the person would run out of apples after a time, while other parts of the orchard might remain full of un-plucked apples. Now, if the person becomes open to traversing across newer paths in the same orchard, they will come across trees that are still laden with fruits and would offer a bountiful supply. Just by seeing further beyond the old-worn paths, the person's 'luck' of finding the fruits increased in this instance while consuming lesser energy to find them. The person turned luckier by embracing newer paths, newer opportunities. The more we tie ourselves to only one kind of living, the more we shut the door to the *luck* that comes crossing our way so very often. The more we keep doing the same activity over and over again, the more sedate we get into that repetitive lifestyle – sidestepping the potential opportunities that might pass by. The more we keep ourselves tied to the same repetitive knowledge, the more we saturate ourselves with it and hence suppress the potentially more enticing & lucrative avenues that may lie out there in the open.

There has to be a reason for everything.

You have chanced upon this book for a reason that life may have presented as an opportunity.

This book imparts all the hydroponic information – all practical, that allows the reader to embark upon a life-transformative journey of lucratively growing veggies without soil – a very profitable commercial venture, or just as a rewarding hobby. This book allows one to become a hobby practitioner of hydroponics as well as to initiate a professional journey toward commercial hydroponics. The book empowers the reader to pursue hydroponics as a secondary, or even primary, occupation, or to just indulge in a beyond the ordinary way of a greenful life – either way, getting future-ready from a climate perspective.

◆◆

Can there be a modicum of possibility that this book reached your hands, not by chance, but effected by the environment? Beyond luck and application of self, is it possible that the environment around us might be playing a role in formulating the path? Can there be any contribution of the environment toward our destiny? Is there a latent power of the environment, shaping everything around us?

Numerous scientific experiments have been conducted to explore this aspect. Very briefly, the gist of a few is presented here. These enigmatic scientific experiments will force one to think about the unknown - that science has been able to seek but not been able to grasp. These are some mind-boggling scientific experiments and truths – which science has discovered but for which science has yet to find the reason. These are presented to buttress the point the book started with, that there's a lot more to life than one can fathom and a lot more to how things happen around us, how opportunities may present… like this book in your hands.

Little do we know, if at all, how the universe operates or how events shape around us. We believe what we see, but there is much more to 'seeing.' I often quote the 'Double-Slit' experiment among my friends when talking about life's mysteries that remain unsolved through *centuries*, even after the application of the best minds. Imagine an experiment that has been routinely conducted for the past 200 years and remains the biggest enigma that never got solved! And probably would remain unsolved forever. Nobody would believe if it was told that our observation – through eyes or mentally – shapes the world around us. 'The Observer Effect' is the term used in scientific circles for it. That's what this experiment is about, since the past 200 years that baffled even the brightest minds, including Einstein, who in an attempt to solve it, is reported to have said, *"There's spooky action at a distance."*

Skipping the technical details, the Double-Slit experiment comprises 2 parallel slits through which light, when passed, behaves differently depending on whether it is being observed or not. That's the primary bafflement – that light behaves differently when it is being observed and differently when it is *not* being observed. When there is no one to observe it, it behaves like a wave, creating interference patterns beyond the slits – exactly as created by interference of the waves. But when any detector is placed to observe the phenomenon, light starts behaving like particles, creating patterns beyond the slits as created by the impingement of solid particles. Numerous modifications of the experiment have been conducted, with an 'observer' sitting at a distance, even on a different continent, and yet the same effect occurs. As if light photons know that they are being observed or not – close by or remotely in some other continent. It gets even more baffling when the observation is intended to be done in the future, that is, the observation is intended to be performed 'after' the experiment is conducted – still yielding the same results – as if light photons know that they are going to be observed in the future and behave accordingly in the present. This is all factual, not fantasy. This is something that has remained a mystery in top scientific circles worldwide for the past 200 years – with no explanation except making people wonder for centuries if the eyes and our mind are communicating with light photons! Do our eyes & our conscience influence the environment?

Cleve Backster was an American interrogation specialist, specializing in lie detection for which he created a polygraph equipment for lie detection. One random day, he plugged his polygraph equipment into the leaf of the plant sitting by his study desk to check how much time it takes for the water to reach the leaves. Then, out of curiosity, he thought about how the plant would behave if he were to burn its leaf – and surprise!

Immediately, the readings on his polygraph equipment went berserk – as if the plant could sense there was a plan in place to burn it! He conducted several experiments thereafter to establish the theory that plants could sense our moods and threats.

Cleve's work was inspired by the renowned physicist Jagadish Chandra Bose, who had previously conducted experiments to establish that plants react to certain types of music – a practice that is followed today by some commercial horticulturists.

The objective of mentioning these few mysteries is to make a case that the world as it is shaping around us is more complex than it's evident and its functioning is beyond our current grasp. The environment around us seems to be interacting with our senses in a much more complex manner than just a one way communication. The environment has a mysterious way of presenting opportunities and challenges in our lives, and that's scientifically examined through such experiments as something really happening, not just a conjecture. Our reception or rejection of signals that we receive from the environment shapes the future ahead for ourselves. Going a step further, can it be that the choice may be in our hands to shape the environment around us!

This is a topic where instances are aplenty.

Look out for the Global Consciousness Project called the REG (Random Event Generator) on the internet. We'll cover it only briefly here. This project has been running across more than 100 countries on all continents since 1998. The experiment explores the extended capabilities of the mind that are unexplained by science. Naysayers always remain aplenty, though. The experiment involves hardware REGs sitting in various countries, generating random numbers. The hypothesis here is that events that elicit widespread and collective emotion in large numbers of people may affect the output generated by the REG equipment present in the vicinity. In other words, the objective of the experiment is to find out whether the collective emotions of large groups of people can influence the outcome of the REG Equipment in the vicinity. Miraculously, this ongoing experiment has yielded results far exceeding its own set objectives – repeatedly for decades.

In this REG experiment, random numbers are fed into a central computer that plots and analyses them. Generally, the graphs remain like a placid straight line for months together, but astonishingly, the graphs shoot up *before* some high-intensity event is about to happen somewhere in the near future – as if the REGs have sensed something is about to happen through the collective *advance* hidden emotions of people present around that REG equipment hardware. The graph shot up a full 4 hours before the first plane hit the World Trade Center in 2001. Likewise, it happened again, and the graph pattern changed wildly *before* the assassination of Iran's General Suleimani in 2020, *before* Sai Baba's demise in 2011, *before* the bombing began in Kosovo, *before* Nelson Mandela passed away in 2013. Do the brains of people around that REG equipment somehow know *in advance* the emotions that would unfold in the future? Does a universal energy field hitherto undiscovered by science exist!

Sometime in the previous century, Marilyn Schlitz connected some volunteers to a lie-detector kind of device and started showing them randomly generated images on a computer. These images were in 2 categories – 'boring' and 'emotional'. The volunteers showed less reaction to boring images, obviously, and a significant reaction to emotional or erotic images. As the experiment progressed, astonishingly, the volunteers started to react to emotional images a full 5 seconds *before* those random emotional images appeared before them, while remaining neutral *in advance* to boring images coming up randomly next before them. It was as if their minds unconsciously knew what was going to come up next! This was done repeatedly and with several volunteers, but there's no explanation as to how the volunteers' brains were subconsciously reacting in the right manner *in advance* a few seconds before the random images were to appear in the future!

Such are life's mysteries that seem to suggest our minds have already reacted in advance to what's coming up next. How I wish I knew that future emotion on the stock market in advance. But never mind… bliss lies in achieving rather than in a free lunch!

Quantum biologist Vladimir Poponin, a Russian, demonstrated experimentally that even human DNA is a subject of parapsychology. His study was repeated in the US and appeared as 'The DNA Phantom Effect', wherein the US Army conducted these experiments. They took tissue and blood samples from several volunteers and placed those tissue & blood samples in a separate closed room away from the volunteers. The volunteers were then shown videos that elicited diverse emotions, monitored in the form of physical parameters like heart rate, blood pressure, respiration rate, and perspiration rate. Surprisingly, the same changes were observed in the physical parameter measurements of the tissue/blood samples that were sitting in another room. The results remained the same even when the samples were shifted miles away! It was as if the DNA of a person was communicating among themselves even when separated by a large distance!

In a 10-year experiment conducted at Harvard University, rats were trained to run through a water maze. Successive generations of rats ran faster than their parents and were eventually running 10 times faster than their original ancestors that were 10 years back. Surprisingly, rats of the same lineage in other parts of the world also started running 10 times faster over the ten-year period – as if the enhancements in their cognitive abilities were being communicated through some invisible medium across the continents! Next time you do something better, it may not actually be because of you… pun intended!

All these scientific experiments are shared to emphasize that our mind and surrounding environment are much more complex than science has comprehended so far. The environment around us has mysterious, incomprehensible, and powerful ways. In the first chapter, this book said,

"*Decisions are neither wrong nor right. Decisions are a direction that one chooses. Making those decisions right or wrong is in one's hand to a certain extent, and of course, the environment has an influence.*" I hope you now appreciate the inscrutable complexities of our environment and its ever-present latent impact on our lives. The environment, when appreciated with humility, can be empowering and help a person become a better being.

Who knows what the future has in store for you after you have gone through the hydroponic expertise provided in this book. Perhaps the environment has pointed you in this direction, as it did to me. It's a possibility. Belief does not have proof. Rather, belief exists in the absence of proof. Isn't mankind divided by our individual beliefs of Gods – we have never seen? Still, we believe. Some countries even have it in their instruments, like American dollars say, "In God we Trust." Isn't it astonishing that a large percentage of humanity believes in something that they have never seen and never will! It's a belief that we have all succumbed to. How come belief became so powerful!

Everyone knows DNA. We know for sure that DNA has that famous double helix structure - 2 ladder-type strands twisting around each other. It's iconic. But has anyone actually seen that structure? No, nobody has seen this structure with human eyes, not even with the most powerful microscope ever built. But we 'believe' it because the DNA's double helix structure is corroborated by indirect modeling based on calculations and X-ray diffraction patterns. We believe in the DNA structure through indirect evidence gathered through various other techniques like X-ray crystallography, Nuclear Magnetic Resonance spectroscopy, Atomic Force Microscopy, etc. But humans have never ever seen the DNA structure with human eyes with any microscope, yet we believe it - rightfully so because we accept the scientific approach and models pointing toward it.

What about the atom? Humans have never seen the complete structure of an atom in a single lens, but everyone believes, rather knows, that atoms have a nucleus surrounded by shells where electrons spin around furiously. We have never seen a complete atom structure together because of microscope limitations. When the microscope zooms in to see the atom's nucleus, its electrons go far beyond outside of the biggest possible microscope's field of view. If the nucleus is zoomed in to the size of a pencil tip, its electrons would be in the furthest corner of that room - metaphorically speaking. The nucleus and electrons cannot be seen in a single lens. And when the microscope zooms out to see the full atom, only the nucleus remains visible, and electrons disappear - do not remain visible at all. So, humans have only seen the atom in *parts* and rightfully put together a picture of its structure, a belief backed by scientific evidence *seen* in parts - that the atom structure has a nucleus with electrons spinning around. I've emphasized 'seen' because even 'seeing' is not conclusive, if you recall the Double-slit experiment discussed when starting this discussion.

Kuda Bux was a magician in the past century who devoted his life to learning and meditating under his master's tutelage. Eventually, he could see with his eyes closed! With eyes closed, he could connect with the environment and unravel it better than he could with open eyes. Like 'Hundred Eyes' on Netflix! With eyes closed and blindfolded with layers upon layers of opaque cloth with dough stuffed in between, he could still see 360 degrees – even something kept behind him. Ladies at his London show refused to use the changing room with him around, as they couldn't trust the privacy offered by just a few walls. He even went on to walk numerous times on live burning coal beds, to which his explanation was that he was *'concentrating to such a degree that I see nothing but the fire, and the fire being cold'*. Read this in the context of the Double-slit experiment discussed in the previous paragraph, and I leave it to the reader to ponder if there can be a link.

So, how did the belief in God become so powerful? Let's discuss this in just a paragraph and conclude. We do not have any scientific evidence to back up our belief that God exists; still, the vast majority believes in God, like we believe in the structure of atoms and DNA. Most believers start as part-believers, and the belief in God gets stronger as we course through the stumbles & rumbles of life. We said there's no scientific evidence that God exists and it's only a belief. Let me correct myself. In the context of scientific evidence regarding God, I prefer to subscribe to the thoughts of numerous explorers and historians who have done a wonderful job in putting the dots together, based on scientific evidence available in the form of prehistoric rock engravings. These people have done an astounding amount of research and devoted their entire lives to attempting to solve the God question. These explorers traversed across the face of the Earth in their writings, doing explorations and analysis of the prehistoric remains. All their books and media are worth spending time on. Just after reading a few such books, I am confident that you'll also see the point, that we have proofs all around us that we were visited by Gods not once, but multiple times. Not at one place, but all over the face of the Earth. Prehistoric paintings are cast in stone not at one place, but all the way from Africa to Europe to the USA to Canada. And in Asia too. And all these prehistoric rock carvings from thousands of years ago, spread across continents uniformly, show people dressed in astronaut-type suits and natives bowing before them. Repeat – prehistoric rock carvings showing people dressed in astronaut-type suits – not at one place but similar drawings scattered all over the world. Where would those natives spread across continents, thousands of years back, get inspiration to draw space suits? I know I've put it too directly and too mildly because the intention is not to consume too much time on the subject. So straight to the point. There are remarkable details and substance available, and more than ample proofs exist across the face of the Earth, that the Earth has been visited often by some external beings and those became the precursors to the

Gods that we have today. Having put it simply in a single liner, if you need convincing, do read some such books by authors like Erich Von Daniken or Graham Hancock or the like. You'll not be disappointed.

So, with the belief that the environment has led you to this book for a purpose, please start with hydroponics first as a hobby and then progress toward a professional level after gaining some first-hand exposure. This book aims to make hydroponics a less esoteric art, empowering the reader to practice it at any level, surely, in abundance and very profitably. Remember, hydroponics can provide a really fast payback in just a year!

Wishing you immense hydroponic success.

References

1   Climate change: 'Uncharted territory' fears after record hot March.
    www.bbc.com/news/science-environment-68665166
    www.ndtv.com/world-news/2023-likely-hottest-in-100-000-years-scientists-call-it-a-warning-to-humanity-5016371

2   Morocco drought: Satellite images show the vital Al Massira reservoir is shrinking.
    www.bbc.com/news/world-africa-68665826

3   www.bbc.com/travel/article/20231218-why-olive-oil-prices-are-soaring-and-what-to-do-about-it.

4   'Red gold': Why saffron production is dwindling in India
    www.bbc.com/news/business-67143765.

5   www.timesofindia.indiatimes.com/travel/travel-news/thailand-shuts-down-pling-island-due-to-extensive-coral-bleaching-discovery/articleshow/110004048.cms

6   Taiwan: The 'God Flower' vanishing because of climate change.
    www.bbc.com/news/world-asia-67342419

7   Causes of Climate Change,
     www.epa.gov/climatechange-science/causes-climate-change

8   www.carbonbrief.org/explainer-how-the-rise-and-fall-of-CO_2-
     levels-influenced-the-ice-ages/

9   www.climate.gov/news-features/understanding-climate/
     climate-change-atmospheric-carbon-dioxide.

10   www.energyeducation.ca/encyclopedia/Glacial_and_
     interglacial_periods.

11   Man's Thriving Garden, Sealed in a Bottle, hasn't Been
     Watered in Decades,
     www.weather.com/home-garden/news/thriving-garden-bottle.

12   Earth system impacts of the European arrival and the Great
     Dying in the Americas after 1492
     www.sciencedirect.com/science/article/pii/
     S0277379118307261

13   Breakdown of carbon dioxide, methane, and nitrous oxide
     emissions by sector.
     www.ourworldindata.org/emissions-by-sector

14   www.glassonweb.com/article/modern-glass-facades-air-
     conditioning-and-energy-production-included.

15   Energy Consumption by Country in 2024
     www.worldpopulationreview.com/country-rankings/energy-
     consumption-by-country

16   Future agricultural phosphorus demand according to the
     shared socioeconomic pathways, www.sciencedirect.com/
     science/article/pii/S0959378017308786

17   www.fertilizer.org/news/argus-ifa-study-reaffirms-no-shortage-
     of-phosphate-rock/

18   "Phosphorus use efficiency and fertilizers: future opportunities for improvements," Martin BLACKWELL1, Tegan DARCH1, Richard HASLAM2

19   www.unep.org/news-and-stories/story/methane-emissions-are-driving-climate-change-heres-how-reduce-them.

20   www.statista.com/statistics/647449/average-utilized-agricultural-area-per-greenhouse-horticulture-farm-in-the-netherlands/

21   www.forbes.com/sites/stuartanderson/2023/03/06/indian-immigration-to-canada-has-tripled-since-2013/?sh=6521fabc5620.

22   Electricity consumption per capita worldwide in 2022, by selected countries. www.statista.com/statistics/383633/worldwide-consumption-of-electricity-by-country/

23   Handbook for Vegetable Growers, 1960. Knott, J.E. John Wiley and Sons, Inc.

24   Seeds, The Yearbook of Agriculture, 1961. Stefferud, A. Editor. The US Gov. Printing Office.

25   The 'flying rivers' causing devastating floods in India, www.bbc.com/news/articles/cv2g9x47441o.

Hydroponic Images

If you want to see the following images in color, please scan this QR code.

Commercial DWC system. Plastic sheets to hold water in tanks and covered by planks to hold netpots. Indoor. No GrowLights.

Commercial DWC system on Rooftop. Using thermocol containers. Outdoor.

Commercial NFT system using PVC pipes, on Rooftop. Outdoor.

Commercial NFT multi-tier system using PVC Channels, Indoor. With GrowLights.

Commercial NFT system using PVC Pipes, Indoor.
No GrowLights.

Commercial NFT multi-tier system using PVC Channels, Indoor.
No Growlights.

Lettuce. Commercial NFT system using PVC Channels, Indoor. No GrowLights.

Pak Choy. Commercial NFT system using PVC Pipes, Outdoor.

Tomatoes. Commercial NFT system using PVC Channels, Indoor.
No GrowLights.

Commercial Aeroponic Towers, Indoor.

Flowers, Commercial DWC system, Indoor. With GrowLights.

Leafies. Commercial NFT channels. Indoor. No Growlights.

Tomatoes, Outdoor DWC system in Home Balcony.

Spinach, Outdoor circulating DWC (patented) in Home Balcony.

Flowers,
circulating DWC,
Outdoor balcony.

Gourd, Vines,
Outdoor Media Bed
in Balcony.

Cabbage, Cauliflower, Broccoli in Media Bed, Balcony.

Lettuce, Outdoor DWC system in Balcony.

Lettuce, Outdoor NFT system in Balcony.

Tomatoes, Outdoor DWC system in Gurugram Balcony.

Herbs, Indoor DWC system in summer. With GrowLights.

Assorted Leafies, Indoor DWC system in Roof top Attic.
With GrowLights.

Lettuce, Indoor circulating DWC system (Patented). With GrowLights.

Lettuce, Indoor DWC system in Gurugram. With GrowLights.

Author's Note

It was March 2020 when the Indian government ordered a nationwide lockdown due to COVID. I was in the middle of a job switch, which got stalled indefinitely as COVID caused companies to go bust. Life has surprises in store, that unravel when one least suspects them to surface. After decades of being in the pole position of the Process Design industry, I was suddenly stuck. I had a choice to take up job offers coming from other cities, or to stay put in Gurgaon where my family compulsions required me to be. I chose the latter but had to remain out of service for a year.

I thank my stars, my family, and my blessings that the situation never became even a wee bit of worry. Why wasn't I worried stiff… is something I reflect upon and wonder often! Finance was thankfully not the concern then, but the Gordian Knot lay in how to keep one's gray cells occupied. The void left by the loss of creative engagement can be difficult to fill, potentially & singularly becoming responsible for disquietude.

In the previous 3 years before 2020, I had already been extensively researching & experimenting with hydroponics – as a passion pursued in my hobby time. Several nutrient compositions were already developed & tested thoroughly. This prior groundwork enabled me to utilize the idle time of one year and turn it into my most creative year yet. This was the year when I delved deep into hydroponics and created several novel commercial products for GreenLoop Hydroponics – a company owned by my wife Aparna and which was in low gear until then. Almost all the novel products created during this one year were the first of their kind, with no precedent... like inventions. Until then, the available commercial hydroponic products were extremely difficult to use. That changed with GreenLoop - which allowed the same nutrients of the same strength to be used for all types of plants, for all growth stages of plants. GreenLoop Hydroponic Nutrients became a game changer and bestseller in India, as they totally un-complicated the hydroponic nutrient usage – of course with good results. Associated novel products like FloraPower, Bamboo Plant Food, Indoor Plant Food, Rain Green also came into being, which remain quite popular. Many of these were spurred by queries from my inquisitive and deep-thinking buddies Kamal & Ritesh, where queries led to solutions. Some patented designs were developed, like locally made Adjustable spray nozzles - that displaced the erstwhile omnipresent Chinese nozzles in online markets.

That supposedly difficult-to-be one year became my most ingenious and prolific year ever to create these novel products for GreenLoop – now entirely managed by Aparna while I've reverted to the job I love – to design projects for Process plants.

On hindsight, it was that tiny conversation with my dear nephew Kartik in the year 2017, which became the harbinger of things to come in the coming years. He just introduced the term 'hydroponics' that elicited my interest and eventually prepared me for the tough times ahead. The choice was up to me to walk the path or to turn a deaf ear. I do often wonder if that conversation with Kartik was God's nudge to prepare me for the times ahead.

——◆◆——

About the Author

Vivek Aggarwal is a practicing energy professional, with more than 3 decades of experience. He specializes in Process design of high hazard projects in the energy industry.

He is also the founder of GreenLoop Hydroponics – a company that makes the most popular hydroponic nutrients in India. He developed several bestselling hydroponic products & designs for GreenLoop – a company owned and now managed by his wife, Aparna, who is the co-founder.

He's settled in Gurugram, India, having previously worked far and wide - Singapore, Malaysia, Milan, Paris. He was a permanent resident of Singapore for nearly a decade, thereafter, choosing to return to India to fulfill family obligations. He started and developed Process teams for several companies in India – Petrofac, GS E&C, Simon Carves, Foster Wheeler (Gurgaon), Lummus Technologies - Coker.

Vivek is a Chemical Engineer from IIT-BHU.

He is a Fellow and Chartered Engineer with IChemE-London.

His wife, Aparna, has an M.Phil. in Tissue Culture.

Has sons Vinayak & Mayank, both engineers with software expertise.

Vivek can be reached at vivekaggarwal860@gmail.com